You Can Teach With Success

YOU CAN
TEACH
WITH
SUCCESS

Art/Illustration by Dan Devlin

STANDARD
PUBLISHING
Cincinnati, Ohio

Edited by Karen Brewer
Barbara Bolton, Consultant

The Standard Publishing Company, Cincinnati, Ohio
A division of Standex International Corporation
© 1994 by The Standard Publishing Company

01 00 99 98 97 96 95 94   5 4 3 2 1

Library of Congress Cataloging-in-Publication Data

Schantz, Daniel.
        You can teach with success / by Daniel Schantz.
            p. cm.
        Includes bibliographical references.
        ISBN 0-87403-964-9
            1. Teaching—Handbooks, manuals, etc.   I. Title.
LB1025.3.S33 1994
371.1'02—dc20   93-42577
                                                                      CIP

*To my Christian Education Professor, John Leinbaugh,
with deepest gratitude for his nurture and inspiration.*

And to Central Christian College of the Bible, my Alma Mater.

Contents

Watch out! If you read this chapter something wonderful could happen when you learn about the seven enticements to teaching. For instance you might decide to quit your job at the barrel stave factory and become a teacher.

Or if teaching is not for you, you'll find that out too. Then you won't have to read the rest of this book. You can go golfing and use the book for pressing leaves.

Schoolmarms and Ichabod Crane, Miss Dove, Mr. Chips, To Sir With Love, Paper Chase, Stand and Deliver, and Dead Poets Society—the images of teachers are many and varied. Find out what it's really like to be a teacher in this chapter about roles. Maybe some of these hats will fit you perfectly. And if not, maybe you can get back on at the barrel factory.

"Teaching would be great if it weren't for students," said a noted college teacher. Truth is, teaching *is* students.

In this chapter you will find a thumbnail sketch of every age group. You'll also learn something about yourself—where you've been and what to expect next in life. You might even come to understand your mother-in-law, but let's not look for miracles.

Preparation. It sounds like a synonym for work. But preparation saves you work and saves your fingernails and your sanity. In this chapter you will learn about a plan to make preparation presto and pleasurable.

Some teachers teach like a surgeon working in total darkness; they're guessing, and it can be fatal, not only to the patient but to the doctor.

Turn on the lights by having a plan and following it. Get acquainted with a tried-and-true-but-flexible plan you can use with confidence.

Remember when you bought that one-size-fits-all shirt and it turned out to be one-size-fits-none? It's the same with teaching methods. No one method works in all situations. Learn about a variety of useful teaching techniques and how to decide which ones to use in which situations. And maybe you can use that shirt to clean the chalkboard.

Chapter 7　The Visual Advantage

You want your students to go to Heaven, but how do you get this across? Draw a map!

If teachers have one overriding fault, it's this: they talk too much. Talk less and teach more by using audio visuals. In this chapter you'll learn about some of the new technology and why the old standbys are still standing.

The good news? You won't have to sell your house to afford visuals.

Chapter 8　Room Service

You wouldn't serve a porterhouse steak on a paper napkin. You wouldn't wear cutoffs to a wedding. Poor packaging. It can diminish a fine product.

A teacher's classroom is his package. In this chapter you will find out how to enhance your teaching by giving a little attention and affection to your classroom.

Chapter 9　Taking Your Temperature

Evaluation—the dreaded "E" word. But wait! Evaluation may be your very best friend. Unless you are the world's worst teacher, evaluation may be the very thing that can change you from an OK teacher into a great instructor. Find out how to evaluate in a painless and purposeful way. Reproducible forms are provided here for your convenience.

Chapter 10　Special Teaching Situations

Remember that junior high teacher who taught you how to multiply fractions, then gave you a test over decimals? Me too.

Some teachers learn to teach in Sunday school and then get

pushed into other kinds of teaching for which they are not pre-pared such as Vacation Bible School or home Bible studies. In this chapter you will learn about the differences in the types of teaching and how you can cope with those differences.

Chapter 11 Emotions, Who Needs Them?

Spock makes a great character on Star Trek, but who would want him for a teacher? Not me.

Give me a teacher with a heart. But with heart comes hurt—hurt that can discourage even good teachers. In this chapter find out how to make emotions work for you instead of against you.

Chapter 12 The Creative Teacher

"All things are full of weariness," said an ancient teacher, and we all know what he's talking about. Well, maybe teaching isn't full of weariness, but it certainly has its sludgy days.

No matter how much you enjoy teaching, there will come a time when you need a shot of novelty to rejuvenate your tired spirit. Learn how to give yourself injections of ideas that will bust the ruts you're in and make you a teacher students can't wait to be around.

Resources

Chapter 1

"*What, Me Teach?*"

I'm allergic to chalk dust.
I don't know which side of the Bible is up.
Sure, I'll be glad to teach. Nothing to it.

Why You Should Be a Teacher

You ought to be teachers (Hebrews 5:12).

A young lady stopped at my office door and asked, "Can I talk to you for a minute?" In her right hand was a wad of tissues, and her face was damp. She refused to take a seat, as if embarrassed and eager to leave.

"I thought I wanted to be a teacher," she said with a tight voice. "But this first year has been a disaster."

I let her ventilate, and then I asked, "Why did you want to be a teacher?" She was vague about her motivation.

If a teacher does not have good, healthy reasons for teaching, then he or she will probably not last long. Fortunately for my drop-in guest, she found good reasons and returned to teaching with better results.

Here, at the beginning of this book, is the best place for the reader to settle once and for all, "Do I want to teach?" And if so, "Why?"

This opening chapter will rehearse some of the best reasons for becoming a Christian teacher—reasons that will sustain you through the early tribulations of the classroom. See if some of them speak to you.

It's an Honor

Respect those who work hard among you, who are over you in the Lord and who admonish you (1 Thessalonians 5:12).

Teaching is the business that is most like the business of God himself.

When God decided to visit his planet, he could have come in any form that he wanted.

He could have come as a professional basketball player. He would have been nine feet tall with hands as big as baseball gloves and legs like a rabbit. We might have called him "Magic" and we would have worshiped him for his talent and performance. Doubtless he would have had enormous positive influence on millions of young and old alike.

Or he could have come as an actor, filling the big screen with a handsome face. All the girls would have been in love with him, and his spare time would have been spent signing autographs and making appearances.

God could have come as a popular singer, and our mouths and hearts would have been filled with his catchy tunes as we went about our work.

He could have come as President of The World, riding in a limousine and changing the lives of millions with the stroke of a pen.

He could have come as a writer, a talk show host, a Wall Street baron, or an astronaut.

But he didn't.

When God came to earth, he came as a teacher.

To be a teacher is to be like God. There is no greater honor.

To Get Smart

Wisdom brightens a man's face (Ecclesiastes 8:1).

Ever wanted to feel smart? To know the Bible? To understand people? Then teaching is your ticket. No one learns as much as a teacher. "To teach is to learn twice," said Joseph Joubert. Just learning for the sake of learning is not the same as learning something with the intent of teaching others what you've learned. As the illustration shows, there is memory leakage when you are just "learning." But when you learn material and translate it into a lesson, you reinforce the material in a special, unforgettable way.

Furthermore, learning with a view toward instruction gives a

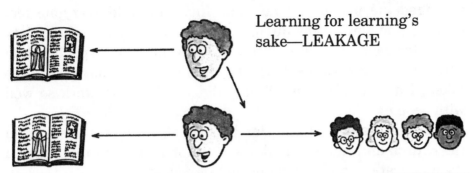

Learning for learning's sake—LEAKAGE

Learning for teaching's sake—RETENTION

learner a special grasp of a subject. Indeed, it could be argued that you don't really understand a subject until you are able to explain it to someone else.

One afternoon I received a phone call from a neighbor lady. "My daughter is having trouble with her science workbook. She doesn't understand the cycles of the moon. Could you drop by and help her?"

"Sure," I replied, thinking what a snap this would be to help a grade school girl with her workbook.

I sat on the neighbor's porch for more than an hour, reviewing the workbook and trying to figure out what I thought I already knew. Finally, with beads of sweat on my brow, I figured it out and explained it to the girl. When I got home I realized that I now understood the cycles of the moon correctly for the first time in my life. I had *learned* those cycles in grade school, but now that I had taught them to a neighbor, I *knew* them.

As a teacher, you will not only learn the Scriptures, but in the process of teaching them, they will become dear to you personally. You will begin to have a sense of proprietary joy about certain passages. "This is my favorite psalm. This is a proverb I love. This is the passage I struggled to explain to my students." Like a jewel in your apron pocket or a trophy on your mantle, the Bible will become your unique, personal treasure.

You will also learn more than just information. You will develop skills and attitudes that will carry over into other areas of your life. You will develop organizational skills, listening skills, and social graces. You will learn to use audiovisuals and other teaching tools. These aptitudes will help make you a better parent, mate, and citizen of your community.

Our local church was putting together a pictorial directory. My wife, Sharon, and I sat in the hall waiting our turn at the camera. I couldn't help noticing with what skill the photographer managed the people he was shooting. He made everyone feel relaxed and important during what is usually a high-anxiety ordeal for most of us. Even little babies seemed to respond to him better than they did to their own mothers. After our photo was taken, I asked this man, "Where did you learn to work so well with people?"

He smiled and replied, "Sunday school, I guess. I grew up in the church and taught Sunday school for several years. It was a great education in the management of people."

His answer did not surprise me for I have seen how teaching can give a person self-confidence, good manners, and a winsome personality.

It's Just Plain Fun

You are our glory and joy (1 Thessalonians 2:20).

We all hear so much from the media about problem students and classroom tensions that it's easy to forget all the good times teachers have with most students.

Take friendships, for example. For several years my wife taught a women's Bible study that met in homes. The friendships she established in that class are still a vital part of her life. She still gets letters and cards from those ladies, and some of them call or drop by just to chat or to get some advice.

The relationship between students and teachers is unique. Remember how it was when you were in grade school? You had at least one teacher you loved. Whenever you were downtown shopping with your mother and you happened to meet your teacher in the store, you lit up with pride and joy. "Mommy, there's my teacher!" We tend to love those who give so much to us.

I remember my college teachers with a kind of reverence. I still write or call them for advice, or just to say hello.

From my own twenty-six years of Christian college teaching I have built a mental file of happy memories in and out of the classroom. I also have a large box full of letters and notes I've received from students through the years. When I get discouraged, I reach in and get a handful of them to remind myself that my work has not been without merit.

I enjoy being around young people because they are so alive. They have a fresh, eager outlook on life that makes me feel young again just to be around them. They are creative, smart, and funny, but also sensitive and sweet. They seem to know when I'm hurting, and they are quick to encourage me. They are quick to hug me or to give me a verbal boost when they think I need it.

Sometimes students pull practical jokes. Although they can be a nuisance, they are also funny and provide an opportunity for teaching and for displaying Christian character.

One time my students filled my office to the ceiling with wadded-up newspapers. At first sight I nearly collapsed with dismay. Then I grabbed a couple students and together we dragged the papers down the hall and filled the dean's office with them.

Former students are like family to me. They often write or drop by to chat. One of them sends me books he thinks I will like, others send pretzels (my favorite snack), and one of them made a lifetime dream come true by urging me to take flying lessons at his expense.

The greatest joy a teacher can have is to see his students go on to be successful in their careers and families. And, although no one teacher can take all the credit for that success, still there is joy in knowing that you contributed to your students' happiness and worth.

Yes, there are some students who disappoint. There are some who cause you grief and seem to fight you every step of the way. But there are difficult people in every kind of work. Sometimes even they turn out to be a positive influence for Christ, and ultimately a friend to you too.

It Demonstrates Concern

But the Lord said, "You have been concerned about this vine. . . . Should I not be concerned about that great city?" (Jonah 4:10, 11).

One of the best motives for teaching is mercy. Currently our world is short on mercy. We are guilty of what I call the "Jonah Syndrome" or "pumpkin pity." Millions are interested in being kind to the environment. Daily headlines urge us to save the rain forests, owls, whales, minnows, and even bats. Meanwhile millions of unborn babies are aborted annually, and children are put in mediocre day-care and schools. Scores of others are neglected and abused by their own parents.

It's certainly not wrong to care about cabbages and kittens as long as we give priority to those creatures who are created in the image of God—people like you and me. When Jesus said to Simon Peter, "Do you love me? Feed my lambs," he wasn't talking about farm animals or hay.

Teaching is one of the best ways to show compassion on children, for one of the things children need most is instruction—

painstaking instruction in the Scriptures and guidance on how to live in this complicated world.

Perhaps the teaching you do will save some children from the nightmares of drugs and violence, the swamp of depression, and the tragedy of suicide. Perhaps you can do or say the very thing that will keep a child from the guilt and disease of sexual sin or an untimely divorce later on. Ultimately we want to save our children from Hell and send them to Heaven. But life is long and there are many traps along the road before they get to the end of life.

It's always easier to build children than to repair grown-ups. A little work and sacrifice from you and me now may be worth a lot more than expensive therapy and extensive rehabilitation after the damages are done. The path to God seems to get steeper with every passing year.

And when we think of compassion, let's not forget the adults. Young adults are making lifetime decisions and finishing their schooling. It's tough getting started in these times. Middle-aged adults are bearing the heaviest burdens, caring for children and the elderly, and trying to do it with a body that is beginning to show wear and tear. Many of them, like David and Solomon, find the middle years to be more dangerous than the teen years. Some discover they have feet of clay. Aging adults (who will soon make up almost a third of our population) are facing a series of losses and the specter of eternity. Who will care for them?

A good teacher and a good Sunday school class can be a kind of oasis in the desert of everyday living. You could be the confidant, the friend, the parent, or the coach whom they need to survive the heat of life.

It Pays the Bills

Freely you have received, freely give (Matthew 10:8).

Many of us were born with spiritual silver spoons in our mouths. We live in a country that crackles with religious influences: churches by the score, religious radio and television, Christian bookstores, colleges, day schools, and camps. Some of our states have more churches than entire countries have elsewhere in the world.

For the first twenty-five years of your life you may have been ministered to by dozens of teachers: public school teachers, Sunday school teachers, ministers, coaches, club sponsors, and many others. These people gave up their time and energy so that you would have a chance to go somewhere in life.

So, you and I are up to our earlobes in debt, and I personally don't like to be in debt. I like to pay my bills. When I think of the hard time I gave some of my teachers, I feel that I should be punished! Maybe that's why I don't complain too much when my students give me trouble. I deserve it!

True, you don't have to become a teacher to repay your obligations. In fact, one good way to repay your teachers is simply to use what they taught you, to be a godly person and a good worker in the church. Show them that their work was not in vain.

Even so, someone must replace those teachers who have gone before us. Our parents and grandparents are watching us and hoping that we will step forward and take our turn in the leadership roles of the church. Maybe you have come to the kingdom for "such a time as this."

It Works

So is my word that goes out from my mouth: It will not return to me empty, but will accomplish what I desire and achieve the purpose for which I sent it (Isaiah 55:11).

At times it seems like nothing works anymore. Families are broken. Governments flounder. New cars go right back for repairs. New houses have cracked foundations and faucets that drip. Businesses go under every day. Even sports are corrupted by drugs and dishonesty.

There is one thing that keeps on working, however, and that is the Bible. Isaiah promised that if we teach the Word of God, it will have an effect. It will work!

He did not mean that everyone we teach will be converted. That's unrealistic and denies the free will nature of man. But everyone who is taught the Scriptures is affected, because God will not be ignored. Like sunshine, the Word will warm and brighten our lives, or it will irritate and burn us. But it will not leave us alone.

Sometimes teachers can actually see learning taking place, and this is deeply satisfying. For example, young children are often like hungry baby birds with their spiritual mouths open and their hearts eager to devour Bible stories and songs.

Children believe what they are taught and begin to practice it immediately. One teacher tells about how he urged his students to read the Bible every day. That evening his own daughter invited friends over for a slumber party. Late in the evening this father could hear his daughter upstairs talking, long after she was supposed to go to sleep. Irritated, he sprang up the stairs to reprimand her, but when he peeked into the room, there was his daughter, sitting cross-legged on the bed with her Bible open in her lap. She was reading the Scriptures to her young friends. Red-faced, the father tiptoed back downstairs and said nothing more. She was only doing what he taught her to do.

Those who teach fifth and sixth graders also get to see fruits of their labor, for the average age of conversion is about eleven years. Many of their students are ready for baptism.

Teachers of adults soon see that their students want to learn and share what they have learned. Because they are knee-deep in life, they use the things they learn as soon as they learn them.

On the other hand, teachers of junior high and high schoolers may despair at times because these age groups seem to go out of their way to look disinterested. It's not "in" to be too eager, they think. The average age of Sunday school dropouts is age fourteen. Classes begin to dwindle in size. High schoolers are so involved with activities and schoolwork that they seem to be in a time warp on planet Xenon. For these age groups there is usually a time lag between the time you teach them and the time your teaching takes hold. They may be young marrieds before they remember your teaching and begin to drift back into the church and get involved.

You may not be around to see all the effects of your work, but you can trust the sure Word of God that your efforts are not a waste of time. Teaching is above all an act of faith—faith in God and faith in people. Only God can see the full effect of your teaching down through the years. I was reminded of this once when I was asked to speak at an honor service for a retiring Sunday school teacher in a nearby church. I didn't know the lady personally, but they told me that she had taught the kindergarten class for more than fifty years, so I prepared some general remarks to eulogize teachers of the young. What a surprise to see that the church building was packed with people who came to honor this one wonderful lady. The master of ceremonies began by asking for a show of hands of all those present who had been in her kindergarten class or had children who had been in her class. Nearly eighty percent of the hands went up. Some were leaders in the church. Others had come from several different states to pay tribute to a teacher who had started them off right in her little basement class. For one brief moment I could see a teacher's influence the way God must see it, and I was impressed.

It Has Everlasting Effects

Those who are wise will shine like the brightness of the heavens, and those who lead many to righteousness, like the stars for ever and ever (Daniel 12:3).

There are many interesting and valuable types of work to do in this life. Three of my favorites include gardening, auto repair, and fixing things around the house. Although these activities give me great pleasure and have real worth, I'm not terribly confident that there will be zucchini or rutabagas in Heaven, and I doubt that much of anything will need repair in a world where there is no rust, and everything is incorruptible.

Teaching the Bible, however, has both temporal value and eternal extensions. "Fire will test the quality of each man's

Kayla McClurg, one of my former Sunday school students who went on to become an outstanding public schoolteacher, once sent me the following verse at a time when I was discouraged in my work.

A Teacher Affects Eternity

Do not think
because the light you cast
is firefly soft
and gentle
as the scent of sandalwood
that it does not really
make a difference
in the dark corners
of the world.
You are at its
center,
and so you cannot see
your candle glow
of inspiration
dart its evanescent gleam
down the shadowy corridors
of forever.

—Janet M. Goldstein

work," wrote the apostle Paul. And he added, "If what he has built survives, he will receive his reward" (1 Corinthians 3:13, 14).

Why not try your hand at teaching, a task that the fire of judgment cannot destroy? Then, when the roll is called up yonder, you will hear some of your own students respond with "present."

Is Teaching for Everyone?

Not many of you should presume to be teachers, my brothers, because you know that we who teach will be judged more strictly (James 3:1).

Not everyone should consider being a formal classroom teacher, even though all of us are under the Great Commission and are teaching by our lives. Is there any way to know in advance if teaching would be a mistake for you?

The next chapter, which describes the work of teachers, might give you some clues as to your suitability for the task. But here I offer some suggestions for you to think about in making your decision to teach or not to teach.

Keep in mind that these are *not* judgmental thoughts, meant to keep worthy people from becoming teachers. They are merely questions you should use to search your heart before deciding. Just because you don't become a formal teacher does not mean that you cannot have plenty of good influence in the church, working in some other capacity.

Before You Say Yes to Teaching

1. Am I a Christian? Have I made a decision for Christ? Am I just a brand new Christian? Then perhaps I should wait a while until I am more certain of my doctrine and the workings of the church.

2. What are my motives? Do I want to teach because I like to show off? Am I seeking power, prestige, a title? Do I really want to be a servant?

3. Am I comfortable around people, or am I an extreme introvert who might do a lot better writing articles for the church paper or growing vegetables for the food kitchen?

4. Do I have reason to suspect that people do not appreciate my personality? Do I have a reputation for being difficult? Am I persistently angry, argumentative, obnoxious? If so, then perhaps I ought to join a debate club instead of teaching.

5. Do I have a serious physical or emotional disability that would interfere with my ability to communicate, such as hearing loss or speech impediment? Do I have a medical condition that might frighten or endanger young children?

6. Is my schedule such that I could be consistent in attendance to my class? Do I work the night shift or changing shifts that would cause me to be tired or absent often?

7. Am I unwilling or unable to discipline my own children or the children of others? Since a teacher is responsible for the students in his care, am I willing and able to take that responsibility?

8. Do I have a serious sin problem (such as adultery or crime) that has become public knowledge and that might at this time interfere with my influence? Should I serve in some other capacity for a while or move to another area where my mistakes are not a detriment to my work?

9. Am I willing to make the time commitment to do the job of teaching well? Am I familiar with the local leadership's qualifications for teachers in this congregation?

10. Do I have the kind of gifts that teachers need, such as speaking ability, patience, confidence?

Two Saints in a Silver

"The tongue of the righteous is choice

A teacher once told me that praise is a tool for making people deserve it. "Nothing improves a child's hearing like praise," she said. I thought of her words today when I came across a yellowed manuscript in our attic, a Christmas story scribbled in my own adolescent hand a generation ago. As I skimmed it, my mind drifted back to those high school days at Sabina, Ohio, where I first met Veda and Eva, two teachers in the Sunday school there.

Veda and Eva were two peas in a pod, and the pod was a silver gray Cadillac they practically lived in. If they were well-to-do, they were certainly not selfish. Eva, for example, maintained a large storage closet in the church basement. It bulged with flannelgraph figures, teaching pictures, and books on teaching methods, all purchased from her own purse.

It was their generosity with words, however, that made a permanent plus on my heart. For example, Eva stopped me in the hallway one Sunday morning.

"Danny, how would you like to teach our Primary class sometime?"

I gulped. "Me, teach?" I began to bite my thumbnail.

"Sure, why not? The children would love you."

So, the next Sunday I taught my first Sunday school class, or tried to, but the children looked dazed as I babbled on and on. Many of them wriggled and twisted in their seats, and some actually roamed around the classroom. I prayed for the hands of the clock to move. Meanwhile, Veda and Eva sat at the side of the room, cheering me on with smiles and nods and helping with the discipline. Afterwards, Eva lathered me with sincere praise.

"That was wonderful, Danny. Don't worry about their wiggles. That's just the way they are. I wish I could teach like you, but I'm getting old and out of touch with today's children."

Outwardly I blushed and "pshawed" but inside I gained ten tons of confidence from her praise.

Cadillac

ilver" (PROVERBS 10:20).

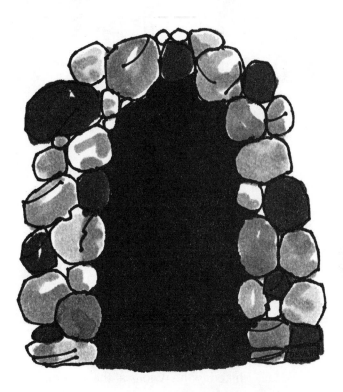

No sooner had I recuperated from my teaching debut than Veda asked me to come up with an idea for a Sunday school attendance contest.

"We need something to lead into Easter Sunday," she explained.

I shrugged. "But I don't know anything about contests!"

"You'll figure out something. You're creative."

In a couple of weeks, I stumbled onto an idea called "Race to the Tomb of Christ," a take-off on Simon Peter's sprint to the sepulcher. To promote the contest I molded a big papier-mache "tomb" and mounted it on the basement wall near the classrooms. Then I fastened a long sheet of butcher paper to the wall, pointing it to the mouth of the tomb. On this I planned to record the progress of each class.

Veda and Eva "oohed and aahed" over the papier-mache "hole" as if I had just made Mammoth Cave out of play dough. "Oh, my, this is wonderful. The boys and girls will love it."

And somehow they did, even though the paper kept falling off the wall and the papier-mache reeked of mildew. Attendance grew, and so did my interest in teaching.

That winter Veda and Eva grew bolder. They asked me to tell the Christmas story to a large assembly of community children.

"We expect one hundred fifty to two hundred children at the church for this event. You are good at storytelling, and the children respond to you. Please say yes."

I said yes, even though my fears said no. Then I set out to write and memorize a twenty-minute version of Joseph-and-Mary-go-to-Bethlehem-on-a-donkey.

Daily I hiked to the woods at the edge of town to practice telling the story to the friendly trees, until I felt I was ready to try it for real.

Sure enough, a multitude of children assembled to hear the Christmas story. I was more confident by this time and did a better job, except for one small detail: somehow I managed to deliver baby Jesus at Nazareth instead of Bethlehem. Never mind. Veda and Eva sat on the front row, smiling, nodding, and sometimes wiping tears from their eyes as I recited my story. When I finished, they leaped to their feet and applauded like two teenagers at a rock concert. Slowly, others began to applaud. It was my first taste of public plaudit, and I made a mental note always to use stories in teaching.

Lest you get the wrong impression, let me assure you that Veda and Eva were not flatterers. They were not manipulating me for their own ends, and they gave advice as well as praise. No, they were sincerely interested in me and showed it by sending me birthday cards and by showing up at my special school events.

My senior year, Veda and Eva invited me to go fishing with them. Next to Sunday school they loved the outdoors. So did I. I can still feel the breathless reverence I experienced riding in their Cadillac, my one and only ride in such to date. No president or king ever felt as high as I during that ride to Rattlesnake Creek.

As we sat on the sun-warmed bank watching our lines, Veda and Eva inquired of my future.

"What do you plan to do when you get out of school, Danny?"

"Oh, I don't know. I've thought about joining the air force or maybe becoming an electrical engineer. I like airplanes and radios."

They smiled politely.

I went on. "Lately, though, I have thought of becoming a preacher. You know, like George Stansberry."

Their eyes lit up.

"He's my favorite," I added. "He makes the gospel interesting and simple."

"We know," they chimed. "You should make a good preacher, but you must always preach like Danny Schantz, not like George Stansberry. God made only one of him and only one of you. No one else will ever be just like you."

I thanked them for their confidence, but inside I harbored self-doubt. I knew I would need Heaven's help to reach my goal.

Then one morning I was wandering through the empty church building, looking for my lost jacket. I started to open the door to the youth classroom, but stopped when I heard voices inside. For a moment I just listened. At once I recognized the voice of Eva. Was it my imagination, or did I distinctly hear her mention my name? I cracked the door and peeked inside. Several ladies were kneeling by their chairs, praying for the upcoming revival. Veda and Eva were among them.

They had prayed for me, by name. It was the ultimate compliment, the masterstroke of encouragement from two sterling saints who knew how to make a somebody out of a nobody.

Like most teenagers would, I took all this encouragement for granted. Now, thirty-five years later, I realize I was being chauffeured into Christian service by two queens in a limousine.

I went on to become a preacher and later a teacher. Every day I teach, I try to tell my students how wonderful they are. When they succeed, I applaud. I pray for them by name and give them important jobs to do. I send them cards and letters and sometimes take them fishing to talk to them of future plans. I'm only doing what I was taught to do by two aging angels who never heard of the generation gap.

Now, if only I had a silver Cadillac . . . .

Chapter 2

The Roles of the Teacher

*A good Sunday school teacher is like a good marriage—a slice of Heaven.
A bad Sunday school teacher is like a bad marriage—
a slice of horror.*

WHAT IS A good teacher? We all know one when we see him or her, but they are not all alike either. Is there a pattern for making Sunday school teachers?

In this chapter we will try to define and illustrate the major roles of a good teacher. Naturally, some teachers are more gifted in certain roles than others, and no teacher has *all* the qualities described in these pages. But most of these characteristics of a good teacher are aptitudes that can be learned and can be improved with study and practice.

The Teacher as a Learner

Some of us have the image of a teacher as a *scholar*—one who knows almost everything about everything. A teacher is someone who reads encyclopedias like comic books and who builds rockets for a hobby. Unfortunately, this image of a teacher frightens away good prospective teachers who know they are only average in cranial capacity.

Basically, the job of a teacher is to *see that learning takes place.* He does not need to be an expert nor even to tell all he knows. What he does need, is to be learning and growing and then to help his class learn too.

So-Called Scholar	Learning Teacher
Has all the answers. Studies to impress students with big words and complicated thoughts.	Knows the lesson for the day, but is willing to admit "I don't know," "I wonder," and "Maybe we can find out."
Is authoritarian. "I'm in charge here, and don't you forget it."	Welcomes input from students, but maintains order and courtesy.
Can't be taught or corrected. Says, "I'm right; don't argue with me."	Says, "I want to be right. Help me find the truth. Correct me when you think I'm wrong."
Emphasizes large quantities of facts and information.	Teaches facts, but seeks to apply truth to real life problems.

Here's a little contrast to show the difference between a so-called *scholar* and a *learning teacher.*

As you can probably guess, the humility and enthusiasm of a *learning teacher* inspires students to learn along with him, whereas the know-it-all attitude of the *scholar* is offensive and counterproductive to learning.

Some examples may help define the difference between these two types of teachers.

I once had a high school literature teacher whom I will call Plain Jane. Jane didn't have a lot going for her. She was not a "looker," and her voice was thin. She was light-years from brilliance. But all of us loved being in her class because of one outstanding trait—her curiosity. She was always asking questions and showing interest in us and the lesson topics, as if she had never heard of these things before.

One day, for example, while reciting, a student referred to pistons in an automobile engine.

"You know," she wondered out loud, "I've always wondered just how a car engine works."

Within seconds, there were four of us boys at the chalkboard drawing diagrams and explaining the workings of an engine.

Needless to say, her interest in our lives and our world caused us to be interested in her world of literature. We *caught* her spirit of inquiry.

Or take the example of my wife's Sunday school teacher, Rick Willis. A compact, handsome man, Rick fits the part of a personnel manager for a nearby corporation. Usually Rick begins class by reading a few clippings from magazines and newspapers, sometimes even with a couple of jokes that have a point. It's obvious that Rick is a reader. Then he gives each class member a handout that outlines his lesson. It's clear that he has studied and has something worthwhile to say. But never is he a know-it-all. When his class gets involved in an intense discussion of some point, Rick listens with the sincerity and concentration of a psychiatrist. Then skillfully, he reconciles different points of view and adds a certain balance to the thoughts. Sometimes he even takes notes on the questions and promises to give the ideas more thought and attention in later lessons.

At times his students feel as if they are teaching him! In this way Rick makes them feel as if they are all learning together instead of one egghead downloading on a roomful of airheads.

The best example of a *learning teacher* is our Lord, the model teacher. Jesus knew everything, but he did not flaunt his knowledge nor beat his students dizzy with information. Instead, he often guided his learners to think through things for themselves, using questions:

"What is written in the Law? How do you read it?"

"Which is easier to say: 'Your sins are forgiven,' or to say, 'Get up and walk'?"

"John's baptism—where did it come from? Was it from Heaven, or from men?"

"Who is my mother, and who are my brothers?"

Yes, Jesus lectured from time to time, but he seemed to prefer conversational type teaching for the most part. Some of his conversations included the woman at the well, the rich young ruler, and the many discussions with the Pharisees. Conversations let the student feel like a part of the learning process, and the teacher does not come across as condescending.

Jesus also used problems and occasions for teaching—the wedding feast, for example, as well as the traders in the temple, the child on his lap, and the upper room foot-washing. In this way students learned with a minimum of formal, authoritarian lecture.

Not only is a good teacher a learner himself, but he also needs to *learn others,* his students. In Shakespeare's time it was proper to say "I will learn thee," rather than "I will teach thee." Thus the emphasis was not on teaching but on learning.

Great teachers always have had a knack for making learning take place without force-feeding students.

Take the example of George Washington Carver, that regal sage of Tuskegee Institute. Carver was a believer in God as well as a scientist. Students often came to his room on Sunday afternoons to talk with him about the relationship between science and the Scriptures. By asking questions and posing situations, Carver *learned* his students to think of nature as a great radio station, broadcasting truth about God to those who are tuned in with curiosity. He used items of nature—plants, chemicals, soil samples—to visualize his points and to reinforce his words.

These informal discussions became so popular that they were later scheduled as regular classes and often had an attendance of 300.

Carver's students felt that they were learning rather than being taught by this humble, godly man. Carver once said, "You can't teach people anything. You can only draw out what is in them."

How does all this apply to Sunday school teaching? How can a teacher *learn* his students? By putting the information into a form that requires students to think and participate, not just listen and leave.

For example, if you are teaching third graders a lesson in God's creation, you might display some nature items (rocks, insects, animals) and provide a tape recording of questions about creation and Scripture references for the students to explore with their Bibles. As the students work at this learning center, you can visit with them informally and relate their ideas and findings to your lesson aim or purpose.

The Teacher as a Model

Here's a scary thought. What if your students turn out to be just like you?

Ouch!

It could happen. Students are always watching you. They notice what you wear, how much food you take at the church dinner, how you drive, how you treat your husband or wife. They hear every word you speak at the church ball game. They even notice little things, like how you sit or stand and if you bite your nails or chew gum.

Now You Try It!

Suppose you have a lesson on the Ten Commandments that you want to get across to your class of Juniors next Sunday. On Friday you catch a cold, and by Sunday you are barely able to speak. How would you teach the Ten Commandments if you couldn't talk very much? See if you can think of three ways. One is given to get you started. At the end of this chapter you will find a list of some other ways to teach the Commandments.

Ten Commandments

1. You shall have no other gods before me.

2. You shall not bow down to [idols] or worship them.

3. You shall not misuse the name of the Lord your God.

4. Remember the Sabbath day by keeping it holy.

5. Honor your father and your mother.

6. You shall not murder.

7. You shall not commit adultery.

8. You shall not steal.

9. You shall not give false testimony against your neighbor.

10. You shall not covet.

Teaching Ideas

Give your class a printed list of the Commandments, and have pupils act them out as charades for the rest of the class to guess.

1.

2.

3.

Yes, it's frightening!

But it's also encouraging because it means that you can have a powerful, positive influence on your students just by living a Christian life. Students also see the good in you, and they even learn valuable lessons from your failures.

In the 1800's there was a college teacher named Mark Hopkins who also served as president of his school, Williams College in Massachusetts. It was a school of about 150 students, most of them awkward country bumpkins. It was located in a mountain valley, so remote that some prospective students couldn't find it, gave up, and went to another school. The campus was crude with unheated dorms and poor lighting. The teachers were poorly trained and equipped. The library was one of the smallest in the country and open only one day a week.

Mark Hopkins was far from the ideal teacher, if judged by the usual standards. He had little training for his work and was not well-read.

He was not much to look at—tall and ungainly with an over-sized nose. He was slow thinking, slow moving, and a little bit lazy. He was shy, partially deaf, and not a great speaker or writer.

Nevertheless, he was a godly man. He was a good father to his ten children and a good husband. He loved the Word of God and loved the young people he taught. In fact, he spent a lot of time just visiting in the dorms and chatting with students. He prayed with them, hugged them, and punished them when they did wrong. When he taught his moral philosophy class, he used the Bible often and he introduced chapel services to American colleges.

In spite of all its disadvantages, Williams College produced a host of outstanding graduates including professors, lawyers, doctors, preachers, newspaper editors, one best-selling novelist, a governor for Massachusetts, and one President of the United States, James Garfield—a Christian president.

Hopkins himself received numerous honorary degrees, guest lectured at Harvard and the Smithsonian, and received lucrative offers from several prestigious colleges and churches. When he was invited to a White House reception for Williams College, President Garfield said, "A log cabin in Ohio, with a wooden bench in it, Mark Hopkins on one end, and I on the other would be college enough for me."

Not bad for a big ugly guy.

Modeling. It's one of the best ways to teach spiritual truth.

How can you be a good model teacher? Here are some suggestions.

Try to be like Christ. Don't consciously model for your students or make an attempt to show off. Just try to be like our model, Jesus, and let students watch you leading a normal Christian life.

Be visible. Come to class early so you can receive your students as they arrive. Hang around after church to visit with them. Show up at your students' ball games and recitals and practices. Visit their schools. Take students with you when you go places. Invite them to your house for sandwiches or pizza. The more they are around you, the more likely they will imitate you.

Be open and honest. Let students look into your heart and see your feelings. Be real. Don't be afraid to let your hair down and confess your inadequacies. If you are too good to be true, they may shy away from using you as a model.

Stick with your class long enough for a relationship to develop between you and your students. It takes time for them to trust you and to begin to pattern their lives after your example.

Are you nervous about the role of a model? Then consider these thoughts.

- You are not the only model your students have. If you fail, they have others to compare with you.
- Students will learn even from your mistakes, just as we all learn from the mistakes of our parents and peers. From the over-talkative we learn to be quiet. From the impatient we learn to be patient.
- Most of your sins are probably "private." Students don't know about them and don't need to know about them.
- Point students to Christ. He is the Ultimate Model. As Paul urged the Corinthians, "Follow my example, as I follow the example of Christ" (1 Corinthians 11:1).
- Your students are still responsible for their own behavior no matter how bad or good their teachers. We are all judged on our own actions before God.

The Teacher as a Lover

Teaching is a kind of love affair—love of God, love of students, love of truth.

A Christian teacher is more than just a merchant of facts. He is more like a gardener of hearts and souls. Without love, students don't respond well to the teacher. With love, even mediocre students often will blossom.

A popular Christian song suggests that "love is something you do," and that's largely true. So, what can a teacher *do* to show love for students?

Teach them. Love does not have to be sentimental or emotional. It can be very practical.

A noted European college teacher was criticized for not being all that fond of young people in his classes. He didn't enjoy them or "get down" with them the way some other teachers did. But he knew his subject, and he knew how to communicate. Doubtless he could have been more effective if he had been more personable, but he taught students what they needed to survive in a competitive world. That in itself is a very loving thing to do.

True, Christian teachers should especially be interested in showing brotherly affection to students, but it's also loving and affectionate to see that they get the whole counsel of God. Students need a balanced, progressive curriculum that will prepare them for service and leadership in the years to come. Teachers who serve only a cafeteria of ala carte electives and greasy fast-food lessons prepared on the way to church are not demonstrating real love.

Curriculum designers have done the hard work for us. But we must stick with a plan, or our students will "graduate" from Sunday school biblically illiterate and unable to solve their problems scripturally.

Be friendly. Always speak to students. Learn their names and use them.

In looking through my file of thank-you notes I've received from students in my twenty-six years of teaching, one theme is constant: "I appreciate the way you always smile and speak to us."

Smiling and speaking are such simple things that we may forget how important they are in creating an approachableness in students. My students reprimand me when they think I've been careless about this.

"I saw you downtown yesterday and I waved, and you never even looked my way. Are you stuck-up or what?"

"Sorry," I confess. "Guess I didn't see you."

Friendliness makes a teacher accessible. What student will come to a teacher with a question or problem if he feels unwelcome or neglected?

One of the finest compliments Jesus ever received was Mark's remark that "the common people heard him gladly." Matthew considered him a "friend of publicans and sinners." People were not afraid to be around Jesus. Even little children were free to approach this God-man without fear. He was a friend to all.

Communicate. Those we love we talk to and listen to often. One of the best ways to build rapport with students is to keep in touch by phone, mail, or with a visit. Mail is a special treat to children who may not ordinarily get much from the postman. Or a mailbox in your classroom can help you keep in touch with those children who are too shy to speak to you in person.

Learning magazine tells about a second grade teacher who was given a girl named Renee. Renee had been abused so badly that she was an instant and constant problem. She swore, threw things, broke things, and just daydreamed her day away. The teacher tried kindness and sympathy, but things only got worse.

One day the teacher set up a cardboard mailbox with a pixie doll beside it. She urged her students to write to Pixie when they had questions or comments, and she explained that Pixie would answer. Of course the students knew it was the teacher who would be answering the questions. But it was a novel idea, and they liked it.

One of the first to put a note in the box was Renee. That began a long correspondence between the teacher and this troubled student. In her notes Renee told things she would not tell anyone face to face. Eventually this one contact with Renee began to change her behavior until she was able to function almost normally in class.

How can you use mail to show concern for students? Here are some suggestions to get you started.

- Remember each student's birthday with a card. Birthdays are big days, especially for children, and they tend to revere those who remember them.
- Send congratulations when you read in the newspaper that one of your students was honored at school, in sports, or in business.
- Send a sympathy note when your student or his family is ill.
- Drop a line of concern to any student who seems to be depressed or upset. "If you need to talk, I'll be glad to listen."
- Calling students on the phone is effective too, and visiting a student at his home may be the "master secret" of good communication.

Barbara Knarr, 1983 third grade Teacher of The Year in Hazelwood, Missouri, begins every school year by visiting each of her students before school even starts. She takes a gift of pencils and a tablet. She talks to students about their own lives rather than about school. She tries to get a look at their rooms, and she admires their possessions while there.

The results have been remarkable. Her children are less afraid of the first day of school, and they are better behaved in the classroom.

It also has become easier for her to confront the parents if there's a problem with a child, because the parents are already friends.

Perhaps these suggestions will get you started, then you will find your own ways of expressing love to your students.

A note of caution: Consider these things a teacher should *not* do in expressing love:

- Don't give treats and favors to students in order to bribe them into liking you.
- Letting students "get away with murder" in your class is not the loving thing to do. Students need order and discipline.
- Avoid anything that might create or encourage romances or crushes between you and students. And, of course, beware of anything sexual or suggestive. That kind of love belongs in marriage.

The Teacher as Motivator

Probably every teacher has at some time wished for a *magic* method or clever trick that would motivate students to learn.

Alas, human beings are much too complex to be "zinged" by one simple approach. There are many "secrets" of motivation. Some of them will work with one student and some with another.

Some of your students are already motivated people. They are smart, energetic, eager to please. They are like whirling wheels that need steering in the right directions.

Some of your students are just waiting for the right incentive to get them going. They are like candles, waiting for the right match to light them.

A few of your students may have little or no motivation to do anything except watch TV, eat, and throw a Frisbee™. Nothing you do or say will change that in some cases. Even Jesus had many who were disinterested in his message, in spite of his wisdom and his miracles.

Although there are many controversial theories of motivation, certain basic principles will work fairly consistently, if anything will work. Here are a few things you might try to "jump start" your students.

Have expectations. Don't be afraid to make reasonable demands on students. Students need challenge, and get bored without it.

It has been observed that Sunday school is "the only school that isn't a school." Why this criticism? Because Sunday school doesn't charge tuition, doesn't require textbooks, doesn't give grades or homework, and no one really graduates. Often teachers don't even take roll, nor do they follow up on absentees. The whole system is shallow and insincere at times.

What can you do to show your students that you expect performance?

Occasionally give an assignment—yes, homework! And be sure to check up on them to see if they did anything about it. Don't make them feel like dirt if they don't respond, but don't be afraid to show a little disappointment and to try another assignment later on.

Always take attendance and follow up on absentees with a card, phone call, or visit. Do this as an interested friend, not as a truant officer. Say, "I missed you, Jill," and not, "Hey, this is the third time you missed my class. Do you plan on going to Heaven?"

Now and then give a little quiz and grade the papers. It doesn't have to be a complex and tedious test. It can be oral, written, or done as a quiz show. Tests show students that you really expect them to listen. They will usually find it fun, in spite of their grumbling. One of the best kinds of tests to give is a pretest before you start a new quarter or section. When students flunk it, they will be ready to listen, realizing how much they need to learn!

One caution: Keep grades private or you may have hurt feelings and dropouts. Let them compete against their own records, not against each other.

Use a project now and then. Give each and every student a specific part to play in the project. For example, suppose you are teaching a lesson about the tabernacle in the wilderness and its symbolic meanings for today. Have the students help you set up the classroom to look like the tabernacle, using cardboard boxes and other castoffs as props. A project like this would involve the artistic types, the energetic, the organizers, and the good readers who would explain the symbolism and read the directions.

Give every student a regular job to do in class. One student takes roll. Another is a greeter. One has the opening prayer. One hands out workbooks, and so forth. Rotate these jobs every month.

Glow! Students tend to catch the spirit of their teachers. When a teacher is truly excited about the lesson and his work, it shows and is contagious. Students can see the enthusiasm in your eyes and posture and hear it in your voice.

So, study your lesson until it grips you—until you can't wait to get to class and teach it. Dress up as if you were going somewhere special (you are!), and get to class early. Talk to early arrivals. Put up a bulletin board display. Use visuals.

When you enjoy teaching, you make it possible for students to enjoy learning.

Praise and correct. Praise is the nuclear power of teaching. Nothing so consistently improves a student's performance like generous praise, and that goes for adults as well as for children.

Students learn by succeeding, and praise is a verbal acknowledgment of that success. Students need help in recognizing their own strengths, and they need the courage to risk learning. Praise gives them this courage and recognition.

The best kind of praise to use is *appreciative praise,* rather than *exaggerated or judgmental praise.* Here's the difference.

Exaggerated Praise

(Use with care. It can create anxiety and embarrassment.)

"This is a *great* paper." (Great? As in George Washington or God?)
"You look *beautiful* today, Judy." (Will she have to look even better next week?)
"This is *fantastic!*" (Really? Is it in the fantasy world?)

Appreciative Praise

(Use generously and freely. It seldom creates anxiety.)

"*I like* the way you work."
"*I'm grateful* to have you in class."
"You *amaze* me."
"*Thanks* for speaking up in class. *I like* your ideas."

There are other good ways to praise students besides verbally. For example:

- Post a student's work on the bulletin board for all to see.
- Ask a student for help in setting up the classroom or visuals.
- Ask students' opinions and advice. "Does this tie look all right with this shirt? Do you know a good place to get my car inspected?"
- Tell the student's parents how much you appreciate his behavior. It will probably get back to the student, and the stealth nature of it will be a plus.

Praise can be overdone to the point of flattery, and flattery is a sin according to the book of Proverbs. Why? Because it can tempt students to be overconfident and proud, followed by a crash. It can even become addictive. Some students won't perform without it. But simple, direct praise is one of the most valuable tools of motivation in a teacher's tool kit. Don't be afraid to use it. Jesus gave his students compliments. Since he did it, so should we.

If praise is food, then correction is medicine. Students need plenty of food, but sometimes a small dose of medicine is in order.

When a student needs correcting, it's best to take him aside and give it in private to avoid public embarrassment. Sandwich the criticism between praise. Show him that you are not rejecting him as a person—only his behavior.

"I like the way you speak up in class. You always seem to have witty things to say. But I'm trying to get some other kids involved in the class, and sometimes you are so quick to speak that others don't have a chance to say anything. So, I'm asking you to hold back a little, please. By the way, I heard you guys won your ball game last night. That must make you feel pretty good!"

Be aware that sometimes rebuke is rejected at first because it is embarrassing, even if done in private. Like vinegar on soda, there may be some fizz and sputter. But wait a while and the mixture will settle down and the behavior will probably improve.

Utilize gifts. The more of your students' gifts and abilities you can involve in your class, the more interested they will be in learning, for obvious reasons.

Use artistic students to help you make visuals. Invite them over for a visual aid party, or hold a before-class session for volunteers.

Use sports fans to keep score when playing Bible baseball and other similar games. Let cheerleaders root for their team.

If you have a nurse in your adult class, ask her to give a brief talk about pain when you are studying the causes of suffering. Have a banker talk about Christian management of money, etc.

Interview college students in your class for a glimpse of the kinds of problems and decisions that have to be made by young adults.

Reward. Rewards have a long and positive history in helping to motivate children to learn. Until children discover the joy of learning for its own sake, they may need a more immediate, visible goal in order to be motivated.

Students can be rewarded for behavior, achievements, or displays of talent. Trophies, certificates, pins, and small toys will give students something to shoot for in addition to mastery of the material.

Some teachers object to rewards, feeling that they are bribes. But a bribe is something you give a person on the sly, before performance to make him behave in a dishonest way. It's manipulative and deceitful.

A reward, however, is something you give a student openly and only *after* the correct performance, as a way of giving honor where honor is due. It's a Biblical principle. We all will be rewarded in Heaven some day. Few of us would last long in the Christian life except that "The hill of Zion yields a thousand sacred sweets before we reach the Heavenly fields" (from the song, "We're Marching to Zion").

True, rewards have some drawbacks and some dangers, but so do all methods. Some students get so attached to rewards that they forget about learning. Then there are jealousies and fightings that always go with honors. To minimize these problems, consider the following suggestions:

- Don't give expensive gifts. Stick with tokens, not treasures.
- Give useful "spiritual" gifts when possible such as Christian books, tapes, calendars, or Bibles.
- Use gag gifts for fun.
- When presenting the gift, stress the work, not the gift.

If rewards are combined with other methods and not overused, they are a valuable tool to teach children the joy of learning.

One final note on motivation. Some teachers use all the right techniques of motivation, but still don't seem to *connect* with students. When this is the case, it's often because teachers are unwittingly doing something that turns students off. It may be something small, such as a mannerism or body odor, but it's enough that they are rejecting you.

For many years I have surveyed my college classes with the question, "What do teachers do that really turns you off?" Here are some of the most common and persistent answers I've received. Note that many of them are small things that teachers can learn to correct.

1. Teachers who come late to class. (This is the single most common turn-off. Perhaps it seems trivial, but it can be an indication that the teacher does not care enough to be there on time.)

2. Teachers who are dogmatic on issues of opinion. (Students like for you to have firm convictions, but they like to have their views respected too.)

3. Teachers who go too slow (boring) or too fast (frustrating).

4. Teachers who always use the same method. (Even great methods get boring after a while.)

5. Teacher who always criticize and never praise.

6. Disorganized lessons and teachers who wander in their thoughts.

7. Unprepared teachers who don't seem to care.

8. Teachers who embarrass or degrade students in front of the class.

9. Teachers who fail to be "human" by always trying to be perfect.

10. Teachers who try too hard and don't allow time for humor, digression, etc.

11. Teachers who repress all discussion, unconsciously or deliberately.

12. Teachers who ignore raised hands.

13. Teachers who complain about the church, the board, the curriculum, etc.

14. Poorly dressed or unclean teachers.

15. Teachers who let the students run the class and have no discipline or order.

The Teacher as Boss

The term "boss" has picked up negative overtones in recent years. Someone who is bossy is someone who is overbearing. Husbands jokingly refer to their wives as "the boss," meaning "hard to please." But the term boss comes from the Dutch word for "master or supervisor." It means someone who has earned his right to be in charge because he is good. Teenagers use the word appropriately when they refer to a car or a singer as boss, meaning "the best."

Every organization needs a boss—someone who will take charge, get things going, and assume responsibility for what happens. A Sunday school class is just such an organization.

To be a boss means to take responsibility for the behavior of those in your charge—in this case, students rather than employees. We call this kind of bossing "discipline," and it's probably the most common problem teachers face.

Some teachers resent having to discipline students. They feel that, "I'm here to teach, not to play policeman." But discipline *is* teaching, perhaps the very best kind of teaching. Discipline is at the very core of Christian growth. If you can help students learn to control their passions and moods, then you have done them a service that will bless them for a lifetime.

Why is discipline important?

Order creates opportunity for learning. Children are by nature anarchists. They thrive on chaos. Leave them alone and they will soon get into mischief, as if commanded to misbehave. (Adults are not always so orderly either!)

When a whole class is chaotic, no one can hear the teacher, and very little learning takes place. Although a quiet classroom does not guarantee that learning is taking place, it definitely increases the chances of a teacher getting through to students. Even informal projects and learning centers need a certain amount of order to be effective.

Discipline challenges. Learning takes place best when learners are moderately *pushed* to learn. Too little challenge and students lose interest. Too much challenge (military order) and students rebel. Reasonable discipline helps create the right amount of tension for optimum learning. Students rebel if pushed with a cattle prod or pulled by a rope. Yet students are bored when teachers make no effort whatsoever to manage them. A good teacher will learn to "push students with a pillow" and "pull them with a string."

Marva Collins, a public school teacher in Chicago, made the country sit up and take notice when, frustrated with public schools, she gave up her tenure, cashed in her pension, and started a school of her own in the basement of an old bank building. She salvaged textbooks from school trash bins, used the backs of old worksheets, and broke pencils in half to make them go around.

In spite of this modest beginning, her school is so successful that several hundred students are on a waiting list. She is training other teachers in her techniques.

Her secret? *Challenge.* She does not let students get by with foolishness, making it clear that the business of school is learning, not play. She has seven-year-olds reading Shakespeare and dropouts from public school reading *War and Peace.* Students have to read one book every two weeks, and everyone must write one composition every day. Marva has reminded us all that challenge need not be threatening but can be fun.

Discipline prunes for growth. Students are a lot like plants—they need to be pruned if they are to produce fruit. "He cuts off every branch in me that bears no fruit, while every branch that does bear fruit he prunes so that it will be even more fruitful" (John 15:2).

It seems cruel, cutting off limbs of a tree or pinching off suckers of a tomato plant, but it's the only way to make a plant be all that it can be.

Children need pruning, or their energies go into wasteful "weed" activity. They have attitudes that need to be lopped off, and behavior that needs to be directed into proper channels. Then students will have more and better fruit to offer.

Discipline demonstrates affection. Discipline is a very loving thing to give or to receive. "The Lord disciplines those he loves, and he punishes everyone he accepts as a son" (Hebrews 12:6).

To discipline is to show that you care. When you look back on the best teachers you had in elementary and secondary school, wouldn't you agree that they were teachers who cared that you learned? They cared about you as a person.

They cared that you did not hurt others and yourself. So even though it put them at risk of losing your friendship, they enforced discipline. They loved *you* more than their own popularity. Gareth Reese, one of my college teachers, used to say, "You'll hate me now, but you'll love me later." I didn't hate him, of course, but he was demanding. I do appreciate all that I learned from his rigorous demands.

Nearly all the students I've had to confront through the years have become good friends. The honesty of confrontation may hurt at first, but in the end it makes for better relationships. "Better is open rebuke than hidden love. Wounds from a friend can be trusted" (Proverbs 27:5, 6).

Now, here is an overview of some basic principles of discipline.

1. Decide what you expect from students and tell them those expectations. Don't expect them to read your mind. Other teachers may let them get away with things that infuriate you.

2. Focus on teaching and learning, not on patrolling and punishing. Have lessons prepared so that there is something good going on every minute of the hour, and bad behavior is "crowded out." "Do not be overcome by evil, but overcome evil with good" (Romans 12:21).

3. Build good relationships with students and their parents, so that when you have to correct them, they know you love them.

4. Have an occasional lesson on the subject of behavior, respect for others, reverence for God. Some kids act up because no one has ever explained to them why they should behave and what behaving means.

5. If you have a large class, be sure to enlist adult assistants to help you maintain order. Their very presence will ameliorate many potential problems.

6. If you have to confront a student for a serious problem, do it in private. Sandwich the criticism between praises, and make clear what you will do next if his behavior does not change.

The Ten Commandments

Earlier in this chapter you were asked to think of a variety of ways to teach the Ten Commandments without using many words. Here are some ideas.

1. Put the Commandments on the chalkboard as a matching quiz to see if students can match the first half of each with the second half.

2. Show students the list of Commandments and give them a piece of candy for each one they can memorize and explain.

3. Ask students to rewrite the Commandments in modern street rap.

4. Have students make clay tablets with the Ten Commandments carved on them.

5. Scramble the Commandments and ask students to sort out the puzzle.

6. Show pictures or cartoons of people breaking the Ten Commandments and discuss what happens when we break God's laws.

7. Put a large sheet of paper on the wall and ask students to draw stick figures illustrating the Commandments.

8. Give students a couple of puppets and let them put together a brief play, dramatizing the giving of the Ten Commandments.

9. Put the Commandments on cassette tape and let students add sound effects.

10. Pass out newspapers and have students find examples of people breaking the Ten Commandments and people keeping them.

Don't Look Now But You're Being

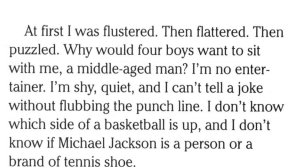

Don't look now, but you are being followed. Those shadows darting in and out of the church pews are children, and they are doing what they do best—imitating you and me. I was reminded of these mini-sleuths last Sunday just as worship was beginning.

You can always find me in an aisle seat because I get claustrophobic with people on both sides of me. That's where I was sitting when someone tapped me on the left shoulder. I stirred from my organ-prelude trance and looked up to see four boys, thirteenish, lined up in my aisle. They grinned at me impishly, and I recognized them as the same boys who had been hanging around me after church for several Sundays.

"Can we sit with you?" their spokesman chirped.

"Well, uh . . . I mean, yes, sure, of course . . ." I nodded to my wife and together we scooted to the dreaded middle section of the pew. The four boys wriggled into the seat and perched beside me like four crows on a fence.

At first I was flustered. Then flattered. Then puzzled. Why would four boys want to sit with me, a middle-aged man? I'm no entertainer. I'm shy, quiet, and I can't tell a joke without flubbing the punch line. I don't know which side of a basketball is up, and I don't know if Michael Jackson is a person or a brand of tennis shoe.

Out of the corner of my eye, I could see the boys watching me out of the corners of their eyes, and it made me nervous. I returned their glances with a mature but friendly smile. They were handsome boys and well behaved. Maybe this wouldn't be so bad.

I'm a good listener, I think. I usually manage to keep my face pointed toward the pulpit and my eyes mostly open. On the other hand, I am very jittery when I'm caged by a crowd. My left earlobe began to itch, and I tugged at it nervously. I shifted in my seat and pried my tie away from my Adam's apple.

So did the boys.

I whispered something important to my wife.

The boys whispered to each other.

The sermon was good but I prayed to be

Followed!

free of this aisle-trap. Out of my coat pocket, I fished a stale mint Lifesaver and sneaked it into my mouth, hoping it would palliate my nerves. It didn't. I cleared my throat, scratched my scalp, and shifted in my seat again and again.

So did the boys.

I took notes on a silent-roll-call card. I winked at a baby girl who was drooling on her mother's shoulder. Suddenly the Lifesaver crunched in my mouth, sounding like a rifle shot as it echoed across the auditorium. My face grew warm, and my wife squinted at me like a mountain lion aiming at a fat gopher. I would hear about this later.

The preacher was on his third point now, but still I was nagged by the question, Why? Why did these boys sit with me? I glanced at them again, and they seemed as comfortable as I was miserable.

Memories of my own youth began replaying in my mind. I thought of all the "older men" I liked to be around in those days. Corky Timbrook, for example. He was a short but powerful deacon who played center field on the church ball team. He could nail a runner from center field with a mere flip of his powerful arm. I thought also of Rich Kees, a handsome man whose beautiful bride was the envy of all the boys. Then I thought of Max Roth, a brilliant electrician who hauled us kids to the Kiamichis in the back of his pickup truck. Last I recalled Eddie Helpinstine, a machinist who rode a motorcycle and loaned me his electric razor to remove my first fuzz.

These were not perfect men. They, too, found church pews confining, and sometimes they even dared to doze. And yet, above all, they were men. Full-grown men who really needed to shave, sometimes twice a day. They were disciplined men, able to make themselves do what they were supposed to do when they were supposed to do it, whether they wanted to or not. Most important, they were there, in church, worshiping God and serving as leaders. Somehow I felt if I could just be around them, I would become like them. I clung like a burr on a pants leg.

48   My wife reached for a songbook, and my memories dissolved. I peeked once more at the boys, and I was no longer nervous. When the minister called out the decision hymn, I stretched up to my full six-foot-one, towering over the boys. I gripped the pew in front of me with masculine hands, and I cleared my throat with a deep, resonant sound. Just to be sure, I brushed my face with my hand to see if I needed a shave.

The service was over now, and I was sadder than usual.

"Thanks for letting us sit with you, Mr. Schantz," the boys chorused, and then they disappeared into the crowd.

"Sure," I mumbled to myself. "Anytime."

I'll never know for certain why those boys shadowed me that morning, but the shadows know, and that's what matters. Two things I do know for certain: we are being watched at all times, and Lifesavers can get you into big trouble.

Chapter 3

Introducing:
Your Students and Their Characteristics

How to Use This Chapter

Bracket the Age

If you already know which age group you plan to teach, then read that section carefully. Next, read the age group that comes *before* that one, so that you will know where your students have just been. Finally, read the section that comes *after* your chosen age group, so you will know where they ought to be when they are finished with your class.

Survey All Ages

If you don't know which age group you want to teach, read all of these descriptions, looking for one that seems to speak to you. Think about the age of people you enjoy in everyday life. That will give you a clue as to where to start.

One of the most common reasons teachers quit teaching is that they are mismatched with an age group. A few teachers can teach almost any age group and be happy and successful. But most of us have a favorite age, and one that is definitely not a favorite. I like almost all age groups except high schoolers. I find them threatening for some reason. But by the time they get to college, I like them.

Note Techniques

As you read these descriptions, pay special attention to how each age likes to be taught. If you are unaware of their special communication needs, you may not be able to reach them, or worse, you may ask them to do something they are not fully capable of doing. Trying to make a tadpole hop is very frustrating.

By the time children reach Junior age they have most of the basic learning skills they need, but there are tremendous differences between the ages, all the way to the end of life. Young adults and older adults, for example, are as different as nursery and high school.

One caution: These descriptions are merely clues to the general nature of each age group. Trying to describe any one age in a few words is like taking a snapshot of a car race—as soon as the picture is taken, the situation has changed. What worked with your class six months ago might suddenly stop working, not because you are doing something wrong, but because your students have changed so much in just six months.

Finally, remember that no two human beings or classes are alike. They are much too complex to pin down with a few generalizations. Students may look pretty much alike, but like salt and sugar or flour and chalk, they look alike but they are intrinsically different. I've taught Junior classes that were textbook in nature—smart, noisy, energetic. And I've taught Junior classes that were quiet little mice and not very bright. Classes have a personalities of their own.

Know Individuals

Even more important than knowing the general characteristics of your chosen age group is getting to know the individuals of your class. You can do that by visiting with them, by interviewing a couple in class each week, or by using a printed questionnaire like the one shown here. (However, you may need to adapt this one to meet the needs of your age group.) Give the questionnaire to class members at the beginning of the year and then to each newcomer throughout the year.

Note to teachers: Fill out a questionnaire yourself, and reproduce it for your students so they can get to know you. Give them yours first so they will see how to answer the questions.

Getting to Know You

Your full name _____

Your nickname or preferred name _____

Address _____

Telephone _____

Describe your family: (parents, brothers, sisters, etc.):

_____

_____

_____

_____

Your favorite school subjects: _____

Your favorite TV shows: _____

Your hobbies or favorite sports: _____

Your favorite magazines and books: _____

Your favorite parts of the Bible: _____

_____

Are you ❑ happy, ❑ sad, ❑ up, or ❑ down most of the time?

Do you like to ❑ listen or ❑ talk most of the time?

Do you like to ❑ be alone or ❑ be with people most of the time?

Are you a member of the church? ❑ yes ❑ no

Who are some people you really like and respect? _____

_____

_____

_____

What do you think are your best skills (art, music, sports, etc.)? _____

_____

_____

_____

Your Signature _____

❑ I don't mind sharing this information with the class except for things marked with an *.

❑ I would rather you not share this information with the class.

Twelve Ages of Life

Tammy Toddler   (Ages 12-24 Months)

I'm one year old and not much to look at, just thirty inches tall and weighing about twenty-five pounds. I can mumble about four words and imitate a few other words with sounds. I can sit alone, stand alone (barely), and sometimes even take a few steps, with a little help. I can feed myself and I can take some of my clothes off, but I'm no good with buttons and zippers.

Although I'm aware of other children in the room, I'm definitely not a groupie. I may be with a group, but I play by myself. I'm wrapped up in my own private little world. "Me" and "Mine" are two of my favorite words. I have a rather sensitive nervous system and I'm easily frightened and frustrated, so be careful how you handle me. My concentration is extremely short and I like to move around a lot, so you'd better have a large room for kids like me.

Sometimes my teachers feel more like baby-sitters than teachers, but let me assure you that I am learning more than they ever imagined. I'm a regular learning machine—a thirsty sponge, soaking up impressions and ideas from everything I touch. I use all my senses, and not always the ones I'm supposed to use. For example, if you hand me a pretty picture I will look at it, smell it, taste it, roll it up and bounce it on the floor, step on it, then pick it up and open it, look at it, and think about it before giving it to someone.

I love to play, and I work harder at play than grownups do at their jobs. You would have to be an Olympic athlete to follow me around and do all that I do in a day's time. From toys I learn about colors and weights, sizes and shapes, motion and balance, and dozens of other things, such as creating, sharing, patience, and pain.

I study my teacher's face like a book, and I can tell when she's in a good mood. I like it when she laughs and when she sings while rocking me. She tells me little stories, and though I don't know what all the words mean, somehow I understand. My favorite is the Christmas story about baby Jesus, but I also like the one about Moses in the basket.

I'm learning some very important words in Sunday school class. Words like "Bible" and "Jesus" and "pray," as well as "good" and "bad," "yes" and "no." I like to hear the same stories over and over and sing the same songs over and over. It makes me feel very secure. And of course, I love cookies and milk, jumping and clapping, crawling and sleeping.

My teacher is very careful to make our time together a happy time. She knows that my experience here will affect my attitude toward church for the rest of my life.

These teachers are so lucky to have me. I'm so cute and precious that I will wrap my arms around their hearts and give them far more joy and love than they give me.

Tina Two-Year-Old   (Ages 2, 3)

At thirty months of age I can get around pretty well. I can walk forward, backward, and sideways, and navigate stairs in my own unique way. I like to do things, like throwing a ball or a pencil, just to see what happens, but I'm not so good at catching things thrown at me.

I like to get into things and try new things like pulling lamp cords or turning on the hot water faucet, but I don't stop to think about the consequences of my actions. I'm just curious and have to experiment.

I have lots of new feelings such as shyness, fear, guilt, and good feelings like confidence and excitement. Sometimes I get frustrated and lose my temper and get in little fights with my brother or my friends. You probably think my favorite word is "No!" It's just that the word "No" seems to get such a response out of adults. Maybe that's why my age is often referred to as "the terrible 2's."

I know about fifty words and I like to babble, but sometimes I get in such a hurry that I stammer or stutter, trying to find the right words. I tend to use telegraphic phrases instead of perfect sentences. "I like doll." "It broked. You fix?" But even though my language is not perfect, I put a lot of "body" into my expressions to help you understand what I mean. If I'm angry, I throw a little tizzy. If I'm bored, I fall asleep. If I'm sick, I throw up. If I'm excited, I wet my pants.

If you want to be my teacher, remember that I lose interest in activities quickly, so you'd better have several things for me to do. I like to hear the same stories and songs over and over. I want to learn about the Bible and God. I like to pray and hear Bible stories. I want to learn to share and to wait my turn, but those are pretty big orders for me at this age.

Perry Preschooler   (Ages 4, 5, Kindergarten)

I'm much bigger and stronger than I was in my nursery days. You'll get tired fast if you try to carry me. Fortunately, I get around by myself pretty well. I can walk, run, jump, and climb stairs. My small muscles (fingers and toes) are still rather immature, so I'm awkward with things like scissors and crayons. I'm mostly a scribbler, and I'm not interested in keeping in the lines. I just want to put some bright colors on the paper. I'm learning to do zippers and buttons, and sometimes I can tie my shoes. Sometimes I can't, too. I'm a very busy little man, but I tire quickly.

I like to ask questions. I'll ask more questions than you and Solomon together could answer. Things like:

"Is the tooth fairy a girl or a boy?"

"If the sun is burning, where is the smoke?"

"Do elephants have belly buttons?"

It's not that I always want answers, although I am very curious. It's more a matter of practicing my language skills and getting your attention. I like the way my questions make you fumble and laugh.

I'm a very trusting person, so be careful that what you tell me is true. If you told me the moon is made of JELL-O, I would believe you. If you leave the room and tell me you will be right back, you had better be right back, or I'll come looking for you.

I play with other children, but I'm still rather egocentric. I like to pretend. I have a couple pretend friends who always do whatever I say. I feel very safe with them.

I'm beginning to think about God and what he's like. You'll be glad to know that he's a lot like you, teacher, and like my Mom and Dad. So be careful what you do and say when you are "being God."

I like it when you read aloud to me. Just being on your lap makes the story so much more interesting.

I like to make things at Sunday school. I like to take my work home for my parents, who always find my work great. I like to go to church. I want to please my parents and my teachers.

Patti Primary   (Ages 6, 7; Grades 1, 2)

I feel really grown up these days, especially since I started school. It was hard, at first, being away from Mom all day, but I have three good friends at school. I have a boyfriend too, but he doesn't know I like him, and I'll never tell.

I like to play with other kids, but sometimes I'm a bit bossy and selfish. I want to be the first and best at everything. Maybe that's why I really don't like competitive activities. They overstress me and I start to cry. My favorite kind of play is imitation. I like to play house and office. I also like to do "real" work, such as helping Mom at the computer or helping Dad wash the truck.

I can handle most of the tools of learning: scissors, pencils, pencil sharpeners, paintbrushes, and I've learned that I'm left-handed. I like to type on the computer, even though it doesn't always come out the way I want it. I like to make things like scrapbooks and valentines and cookies and Christmas presents.

Television is one of my favorite things, but my mom will let me watch only certain things. Sometimes television confuses me. I get Darth Vader and Satan confused. I wonder if Batman is an angel. Where is Indiana Jones in the Bible?

I'm beginning to understand right from wrong, and it makes me sad when I do wrong or see other people do wrong. I have a lot of fears, like the fear of getting lost at the shopping mall (I did!), or fear of going to the dentist, or walking to the library by myself. I worry that I'm not pleasing my mom and dad because I want to please them so much.

I love learning about God in Sunday school, especially about how he watches over us and loves us, even if we're bad. But I'll have to admit that I don't understand some of the songs we sing. What is "a fountain flowing deep and wide"? Our drinking fountain isn't deep and wide. And what is "Kum Ba Yah"? Our teacher told a story about the healing of the ten *leopards,* but Dad said I got it mixed up and that it was *lepers* not *leopards.* I wonder what lepers are.

I suppose the thing I need most at my age is to be loved and accepted by grown-ups. I want to be like them, and someday I want to be a Christian. But I'm not sure what that's all about yet.

Marvin Middler   (Ages 8, 9; Grades 3, 4)

Although I'm growing steadily, it's nothing spectacular at this stage. The girls are growing a little faster than I am, and they are a lot better with artsy-craftsy things. Maybe that's why most of my friends are other guys. I like to play soccer at recess, and I "live" at the swimming pool in the summer.

Girls are OK, but I can see that they are different from us guys. I'm in Cub Scouts, but my sister is in Camp Fire Girls. I like soccer, she likes softball. I like music and science, she likes math and language arts. We both like computers and computer games. From games I am learning all about things like rules and about losing with style and winning with humility.

I read and write fairly well, and I have my own Bible. I like to work in workbooks. I try to see how fast I can get done.

I've recently discovered humor. I know a lot of stupid jokes if you want to hear them. We guys tease each other a lot. We have nicknames for each other. I'm "Starvin' Marvin" because I'm kind of skinny.

I don't like to be treated like a kid, even though I am one. I like challenge, and sometimes I bite off more than I can chew. I like to memorize Bible verses, look up things in the Bible, and act out Bible stories.

Lately I've been feeling a lot of guilt. I guess it's because the more I learn about right and wrong, the more I seem to do wrong. Then I feel bad about it. Whenever my parents argue, I feel especially guilty, like I was the cause of it. Some of my friends' parents are divorced, and I'm scared that my mom and dad will too, even though they say they won't.

I'm beginning to see that life is not so simple and that I just might need a lot of help getting through it. I want to be on God's side, so he will help me safely through life. I've been giving more serious thought to becoming a Christian, but I have a lot of questions. I'm a little bit afraid to ask them.

Jessica Junior   (Ages 10, 11; Grades 5, 6)

You've probably been warned about me, but don't believe everything you hear. Sure, we Juniors are full of "juice," and we make a lot of noise at everything we do—especially the boys. But we can also be quiet and sensitive. We are probably a lot smarter than you imagine, though we don't always show it.

My motto is "Just do it!" I don't want to hear about it or think about it. I want to do it, and that means real things, not just busy work.

I like to compete with my friends, but the boys don't seem to like us girls too much. They keep to themselves. Seems like the boys are always fighting. They are so quick to be offended, then they have to put on a show to prove what *men* they are. They are so daring and rough—always taking chances, racing their bikes, skateboarding down steep hills. And talk about blunt! Boys are truly crude in the things they say.

I tend to have heroes at my age. Most of them are actors, musicians, and athletes. My first loyalty is still to my parents. If you were my teacher, chances are I would put you high on my list of favorite people too.

My parents spend a lot less time with me than they used to. I like the freedom and trust, but I still like some attention from them and other grown-ups sometimes.

I like teachers who have things for me to do, like making posters, or making a video, or making a plaster map of Jerusalem. I like to use maps, and I'd like to know more about the chronology of Bible events like which came first, the exodus or the flood? I love Bible drills and Bible baseball, and I like memorizing Scriptures. I take great pride in my good memory.

I have all the basic tools for learning now. I can reason, and I can understand abstract and symbolic things. If you can explain it, I can understand it. Just be sure to help me with illustrations and visuals.

Right now I have a lot of serious questions about God—like why do bad things happen to good people? It's not that I'm an atheist or that I'm being critical. I really want to know, if there is an answer, that is. Don't laugh at my questions, even if they are funny. I may be just smarting off, but then again I might be asking a real question.

Several of my friends have become Christians, and I'm thinking of being baptized soon. I'm ready, I think. I want to please God and have my sins washed away by the blood of Christ.

Jake Junior High   (Ages 12, 13)

We are the young and the restless. I was not prepared for the changes that are taking place in me. Sometimes I feel that an alien has taken over my body. I've got zits the size of grapefruit, and although my facial skin is very soft, I've got some coarse hair growing on my upper lip. The girls in my class are bigger than I am, just when I am trying to be a real man. They are developing "girl things" too, and that messes with my mind. I think I'm in love with a real pretty girl named Sandra. But all the girls my age seem to be in love with high school guys and have crushes on our youth leader.

I've grown so fast that I can't keep my clothes for long. I hardly can tell where my legs end and my feet begin. I'm like the driver of a compact car who suddenly gets into a full-sized car and doesn't know where the fenders and bumpers are. Dad says I'm a klutz, but I'm not. I've just lost track of my parts.

I am so moody! I have fits of uncontrollable laughter, unplanned belch attacks, gas bombs. I get angry over little things, then hysterically happy, then incredibly sad.

All these physical changes have taken their toll on my social behavior. If you are my teacher, beware. I don't appear to be listening, but I hear you. I just don't have much concentration. Don't blame yourself, and please don't put me down in front of other kids. I already have enough trouble liking myself. Reason with me in private, and always show me that you like me. Stick with me until I get through this crazy time of life. When I grow up, I will remember how you treated me at this age. In spite of all my weirdness, no one has more enthusiasm and good times than I do. Once I decide to trust you, you will find me a joy.

I'm strongly driven by peer pressures, so group activities work best with me. I like informal methods of learning such as discussion, debate, camp-outs, lock-ins, Bible Olympics, and dramas.

Spiritually I have some real doubts, but they are mostly emotional things. Am I in the right church? How do I know the Bible is true? Will I go to Hell if I masturbate? Could I be gay and not know it? What if I go to Heaven and I don't like it? It's not pat answers I need. I just need someone to listen and reassure me that my questions are not stupid.

Heather High School   (Ages 14-17)

I'm sixteen and I look and act very grown up. I've reached full height, and my sanguine temperament is obvious. My appetite is strong, but I'm on a diet. The boys seem to eat all they want and they don't gain an ounce. It doesn't seem fair.

High school is the center of my world. I'm a cheerleader, I play clarinet in the band, and belong to a scholastic club. It's hard for me to say no to any activity, so I'm usually up late at night and get up early in the morning, except on Saturdays.

I do a lot of thinking about life. I keep a journal, and I write some poetry. I wonder about the future, not just my future but the future of the whole world. Sometimes it scares me, but I'm too full of life to hold back out of fear.

Getting my driver's license was so exciting. I have a junker that gets me there. And believe me, I'm on the go, cruising or going to parties and to my part-time job at the bank.

Romance is a big part of my life, but I can't seem to decide between two great guys. Seems like so many guys are always thinking about sex. To them it's like recreation or a game, but I'm turned off by that. I want it to be something special for marriage, but some of the other girls are just as wild as the guys. With all the news about AIDS and other diseases, I think it's more important than ever to wait for marriage. But sometimes I feel like I'm the only girl in school who hasn't "done it."

My school seems to be made up of three cultures—the sports culture for the elite, the academic culture for the brainy types, and then there's the underworld—drugs, porno, cheating, Satan worship, racism, violence. You wouldn't believe what goes on at our school.

When I think about the fact that in no time at all I will be in college, I feel both excited and scared. It will be sad leaving my friends, but at the same time I want to get out on my own. That's normal, isn't it? Thoughts of the future sometimes fill me with panic, and I want to just go out and have all the fun I can before I have to grow up and be sensible. That gets me into trouble.

I want to be involved at church, not just a spectator. I play my clarinet for worship, and I sing in a trio. I like it when the Sunday school teacher discusses real issues with us. I would really like to teach the class once by myself. I could do it, with a little guidance. I enjoy working in the church nursery. The highlight of church was the time our youth group went to Mexico to help build houses and teach the people about Christ.

I need input from adults, including my parents, but I don't like to be *preached* to. Just talk to me like one adult to another, and we will get along just fine. I don't expect you to approve of everything I do and say, but I want you to approve of *me*.

Chris College   (Ages 18-24)

College hit me like a truck. Oh, I love it here, but the workload is awesome. I was valedictorian of my high school class, but I'm doing only average work in college.

Sometimes I actually envy the guys who went to work right out of high school or the guys who went into the service and have all their bills paid by the government.

I'm an adult, physically, but I've got a lot to learn. Never thought I would admit that! I don't take care of my body the way I should. I stay up late and eat like a goat. I broke my ankle in basketball, and that ended the happiest thing I had going. Seems like half my friends are on crutches or have mono. It's hard to stay sane, living in a dorm, and often I get depressed by all the constant pressure of people around me. Today I was thinking, "I just want college to be over so I can get on with my life. I've been in school for the past sixteen years, counting kindergarten. Will it ever end?"

Money is a big problem. Even with grants and scholarships I can't keep up with tuition raises, and last month I "dinged" my car to the tune of two grand. My part-time job pays peanuts.

I spend far too much time worrying about the future. "Will there be job openings when I get out?" "Did I choose the right field?" "What is God's will for me?"

My biggest worry is Jerri. I'm crazy about her. I'd like to marry her, but I can't afford it.

Sunday is a bad day for me, and I feel guilty about it. After being in classes all week, the thought of sitting in a Sunday school class doesn't exactly fill me with tingles. Often I sleep in. When I do go, I prefer to go to just a regular adult class, if only to get away from my peers for a while. I go to the Christian Campus House occasionally, but frankly I'm so "wired" with homework and projects that I'm not doing much for God. That's another reason I wish I was out of this place and into a normal life schedule.

I think what I really need is a dormitory Bible study or a prayer breakfast in the commons—something I can tap into without a major change of my busy schedule.

When I feel that I'm neglecting God, I try to console myself with the fact that college doesn't last forever. Nevertheless, I covet your prayers and friendship throughout this tense time of life.

Yvonne Young Adult   (Ages 25-35)

I never dreamed that I would be divorced at twenty-nine, but here I am, all alone. Never mind the ugly details. I have to go on with my life, but I secretly wonder if my minister was right when he said, "A divorce is never over." What a cheerful guy.

But, in a way, I like being independent again. It's easier than trying to please someone difficult, but I hardly have any time to breathe. I feel trapped by my low-paying bank job, but how can I get new training at my age? I've got two daughters. I've got house payments, car payments, insurances, utilities. And I'd like to send my girls to college someday.

I guess my life could be summed up in one word—*busy!* I'm so organized I feel like a robot. Everything is scheduled, except for my house. It's a mess. When do I clean it?

I know it's no different with my married friends. I hear them complain about not having enough time and money.

I hate taking money from Dad, even though he's so good about it. I want to grow up and be responsible.

I need friends terribly, but it's hard to find time for them. I do have a little telephone network, and Sally and I do lunch one day a week. I have two married couples who come over once a month. The men are good about helping me fix things around the house and maintaining my car.

The church is a big part of my life right now. I want my girls in Sunday school. I need to talk to the minister at times, and I need the fellowship of seeing a lot of Christian people coping with their problems.

My Sunday school class meets a real need. Our teacher lets us open up and talk about our real immediate needs. Then he skill-fully guides the conversation to Biblical answers. He always has a nice handout I can put in my purse and read further during the week. He's good about selecting topics that we are really interested in. It's almost as if he were following me around and knew my needs. He probably has a book or something. Whatever his method, I appreciate it.

I haven't given up on the idea of remarriage. I keep my eyes and ears open and stay visible. But reality is rather stark and threatening at times. I have to deal with facts, not wishes.

I'm just grateful I have a lot of energy and good health and a nice church home to support me. I know that God loves me. My Sunday school teacher said that God will never leave us or for-sake us, and that's a comforting thought.

Max Middle-Ager   (Ages 36-65)

It's funny, but I used to think that people who were forty-five were *old*. And it's true that I don't always recognize the man in the mirror. My hair is mostly in back. I have an extra chin and too much stomach. I would be lying if I said these changes didn't bother me, but the thing that bothers me most, I guess, is the lack of energy. I just can't work the kind of days I did when I was thirty. And yet, surprisingly, I get more done than ever. Better organization and discipline, I think. I work smarter, not harder.

I had my first operation recently—a double hernia, and Lana has had her gall bladder out, but actually we are in good shape. Except for low energy, I don't really feel that much different from when I was thirty-five.

In many ways I'm happier now than when I was young. Young people are always striving to prove themselves and driving them-selves too hard. I have more confidence now because I've

Which Sometimes Acts Worse Tha

A dults ought to act like adults, but sometimes they act worse than two-year-olds. When they do, it's often harder to tame them than it is to quiet a class of toddlers. Here are some of the behavior problems that occur in adult classes and some pointers on how to solve them.

Tardy Tammy

Some adult classes resemble an airport, with people arriving and departing throughout the hour. Tardiness is a way of life with some people—even a badge of honor with them. Mostly, though, it's just a bad habit they have fallen into, although I suspect some enjoy the attention they get from being late. Since the first part of the lesson hour is often crucial, tardiness can be more than just a nuisance. It may become a real threat to learning.

What can the teacher do about tardiness? One, he can establish a reputation for starting on time himself, whether or not everyone is present. This sends a message to the foot-draggers that this teacher means business about learning. Two, he can arrange the class-room chairs so that latecomers don't have to tiptoe through a forest of legs to find a seat. He should encourage early arrivals to sit near the front, leaving back rows for the slow ones.

If the teacher knows in advance that a certain student will be arriving late, he may want to mention it to the class so they will not be swivel-heading when he arrives. The noted preacher Charles Spurgeon taught his swivel-heading audience a lesson on this one Sunday by saying something like this: "So that you all will not have to turn around and look, I will describe to you the man who just walked in the door." Then he described the man in great detail. Point made!

If these measures do not solve the problem, the teacher may need to confront the worst offenders in person and request their help. Give the latecomer a job that requires him to be there early—a job such as passing out quarterlies or taking the roll.

Class

he 2-Year-Olds

Fred Fidget

Just as irksome as the habitual tardy student is the one who is always "stepping out." True, there are legitimate reasons for this kind of behavior. Some adults have medical problems that require visits to the restroom. One Sunday I visited an older men's class and watched as a total of seven men left at different times to use the restroom. Perhaps the teacher should not have served coffee before class! Other students may need to leave early because they are serving as greeters or because they need to prepare for special music.

What can a teacher do about these parades? One, he can let the class know how he feels about these kinds of interruptions. Some students are simply not aware of the noise or disturbance they make. They must be gently told. Appeal to their respect for God's Word and other learners. Two, the teacher can design his class so that there are "informal" times during which the "fidgets" can move around with a minimum of distractions. One teacher I know inserts a few minutes of discussion at the middle of each lecture so the restless ones can squirm without destroying the class. Three, when a teacher knows certain students must leave early, he can alert the class at the start. For example, "Molly will be leaving early today because she is singing in the choir." That way the other students don't have to wonder if Molly left because she was angry, or sick, or bored.

Ralph Racket

Some classes have a constant background din caused by foot-shufflers, quarterly-crinklers, chair-squeakers, snickerers, sniffers, and nose-blowers. This problem is compounded today because many classes meet in unusual settings: park pavilions, mobile homes, beaches, and even in hallways or kitchens. These settings create a grab bag of noises such as background music, wind and weather, and machinery noises. Recently I sat in a basement class made from movable partitions arranged in a U shape. Throughout the hour, ladies walked by with dishes for the church dinner or headed for the restroom about eight feet from where I sat. A telephone at the classroom entrance rang three times during the class hour. Obviously, I learned little that morning.

Some of the racket that distracts the class may be prevented by preparing the classroom in advance. Carpet and curtains may be installed to absorb sound, squeaky chairs repaired, or humming fluorescent bulbs replaced.

If the class is meeting in an unusual setting, the teacher should arrive early and study the situation for perils such as wind that will blow his notes away or a nearby machine that will kick on at just the wrong time. If he teaches a large class, he may need to consider installing a public address system.

Increasing the use of visuals may help the learners in a noisy room. That way everything doesn't depend on the students' sense of hearing. Whatever he does, the teacher should avoid trying to out-shout background sounds. Better to pause and wait for the noise to subside. A popular TV commercial puts it something this: "If you want to get someone's attention, try whispering."

Emotional Erma

Erma is crying again. The teacher said something sad and out came her hanky. Erma has tear ducts the size of coke bottles. Everyone wonders if she is having personal problems of some sort, is ill, or is on the edge of a nervous breakdown. Erma is not the only emotional type in the typical classroom. Moody Marvin is being gloomy again. "We're all going to die in a nuclear war, so what's the use of going on," he says. And Personal Pattie is telling us about her marital difficulties. It's a temptation for teachers to despise these emotional types, but he should resist. Emotions are important dynamics of learning and must be controlled, not quelled. Emotions are nothing to fear. The rule is, "Easy come, easy go." Emotions always settle down in time.

The wise teacher needs to give students help in distinguishing between facts and feelings. The teacher, after all, is responsible for what goes on in his class. If he allows the emotional types to run away with the hour, he may scare away other students. It's important for him to keep the class moving along with the lesson, not floating around in a sea of emotions. He can do this with statements such as, "I know it seems at times as if the world is falling apart, but let's remember God is in control." Or, "Thanks for your comments. I understand how you feel. Now let's look at verse twenty-five of our text." The teacher will appreciate these emotional types on days when they contribute rich enthusiasm and lively humor, or when they pay him warm compliments about his teaching!

Wally Weirdo

Many classes seem to have at least one student who raises a lot of eyebrows with his off-the-wall remarks. Wally may be the man who believes everybody is a communist spy or a Nazi and says, "America has five years to go." Wally may be the soapbox politician of the class. Or Wally may be the one-note person who thinks tithing is the only doctrine in the Bible and who works it into every discussion. Wally may even be a long-winded storyteller whose tall tales bore the class.

The teacher must remember that Wally has as much right to his opinions as anyone else in the class, no matter how off-beat he sounds. The teacher can look for the essence of what he says and relate that to the lesson. He may have to be frank and firm with Wally, but should never retaliate or laugh at him. Try instead to keep the discussion centered on ideas and issues and not personalities. Others may be better suited to answer Wally, so involve them in the discussion.

Some Final Tips

1. Behavioral problems in the classroom often reflect the teacher's behavior. Students may only be imitating the teacher's moodiness, silliness, or sloppy manners. Teachers must take care to dress with dignity and to model the kind of behavior they expect from their students. They must remain courteous and self-controlled at all times.

2. Respect the "speed limit" of teaching. When you try to accomplish too much too quickly, you become irritable. Students need time to digest and discuss the lesson. Involved students are behaved students.

3. Be understanding. Many adults are going through "passages" of life that put stress on them. Cultivate a good relationship with them outside of class, and in class behavior will be easier to control.

achieved a few things. I've got my own construction business. I've got three good kids and have a decent marriage. I'm an elder in the church. I understand life much better, and I don't spend too much time fighting the facts of life.

Oh, I did go through a couple years of real turmoil right after the kids left home. Mid-life crisis, I suppose. I thought a lot about younger women, considered changing careers, got mad at myself for not making more money. I went to a counselor, kicking and screaming, but now I'm glad I went.

My biggest worry is how I'm going to afford retirement. I've decided that if I have to, I will just work until I die. And I worry about how to take care of my aging parents, especially because I don't get along with them all that well.

My faith has taken a bit of a beating by the stress of mid-life, but I still believe the same things, basically. Only I'm more understanding of people who don't live up to the ideal. I know now how hard it is to be good. We all make mistakes, but most of them heal, and we go on with life.

I teach the young adult Sunday school class, and I thrive on it. I need the attention and affection the students give me. They often come to Lana and me for advice about parenting or getting along with bosses and spouses. I feel that I'm really able to help them. Oh, I wish sometimes that I could take a few Sundays off and just sit in a class myself, but most of the time I would be bored by that. I need to be a leader, not just a listener.

You might think that at my age I would be fairly free of temptations—so mature and all that. Not so. I remember that both David and Solomon fell into sexual sin at my age, and it would be so easy to cheat on my business account and taxes. In some ways, this is a more dangerous time in my life than the teen years were. I find myself often on my knees, asking for God's help. People trust me and expect so much out of me. Sometimes I just want to say, "I'm just a person, not a workhorse or a saint. Give me a break! I can't be the perfect person you want me to be."

I try to get away and do a little fishing now and then, and Lana and I walk a lot, trying to keep stress down. Actually, if I can keep my health, then the next twenty years of my life could be the most enjoyable and most productive of all. I have an elderly friend who says, "All the sugar is in the bottom of the cup." I think I know what she is talking about.

Sarah Senior Citizen   (Ages 65-   )

As a young person I used to have a terrible dread of getting old. It looked like a curse, a living death. Well, it isn't that bad. Oh, sure, I have had some losses. My husband is gone. My looks went years ago, but in some ways that's a relief. I used to spend so much time and energy on primping. I have this persistent arthritis, but I have my medicine for rough times. I miss some of my dear friends who have passed away.

But the surprise is that I am still *me*. I am the same person I was at sixteen, only a lot wiser and better behaved.

I like having more time to do the things I like instead of having to prepare meals for family and lessons for my students. I like having a leisurely breakfast on the front porch and slow strolls through the park at dusk. I like letter-writing and reading and traveling by bus with my senior group.

And I have my memories. Funny how I'm able to screen out the bad ones and keep the happy ones fresh and alive.

My children live close enough that they drop by to visit, and my grandchildren . . . I enjoy them more than I enjoyed my own kids! And students from my school teaching days drop in every once in a while. It does my soul good to see what they've done with the training I gave them.

I do worry so about our country. Things have changed so much since my childhood on the farm. I like some of the changes. I like my television, my dishwasher, my air conditioning. But I'm truly frightened by the increase of crime and the coming of foreign religions to America. I worry about the young people. How will they make it in these times of divorce, sexual disease, and rapid change?

There I go again, sounding pessimistic. I learned a long time ago that pessimism is a dead end because it leaves God out of the picture. I will trust God to help our society find its way again. My church provides meaning to my life, although I'm not able to go to evening worship and some of the special activities. But I'm always there for my Sunday school class and morning worship.

My Sunday school teacher is the preacher's wife. She has a lot to learn, but she is a good listener and is very sincere and sweet. I appreciate that. Sometimes I feel sorry for her because we are not a well-disciplined class. Sometimes we talk aloud like a bunch of junior high girls, and we are certainly an opinionated group! I don't know how she puts up with us. But I guess she realizes that we *need* to talk, even if we don't always stick with the formal lesson. We've heard the formal lessons a thousand times.

Now that some of my friends have died, I think more about Heaven and sometimes about Hell. I'll admit I'm reluctant to leave this beautiful world, even with all its problems. I think about my life and my achievements, and I wonder if God is pleased. I hope so, because I have depended upon him to help me through each day, and I've counted on him to forgive my failures and to repair my mistakes. I've learned to love God and trust him, and I'm counting on his loving nature to see me through to the end. If he can make this beautiful world, he can make another one and give me a new body to enjoy it with. That will be wonderful!

Chapter 4

Getting Ready to Teach

Being wise is better than being strong;
yes, knowledge is more important than strength.
—Proverbs 24:5 (*Today's English Version*)

Getting Organized

SMART TEACHERS TAKE an hour or two at the beginning of each quarter to plan their approach. Why?

Planning reduces anxiety. The more you know about the upcoming lessons the more confident you will feel. Anxiety thrives on vagueness and uncertainty. Furthermore, planning ahead will decrease the chances of last-minute panic because you have taken the time to anticipate needs and problems. For example, one teacher was very disappointed and angry because he spent all week studying his lesson only to find out on Sunday that a college team was visiting, and Bible college students were teaching all the lessons. Had he checked the calendar he would not have "wasted" a week's work.

Planning saves time. Sure, planning takes a little time at the beginning, but in the long run it saves many hours of last-minute rushing about. You might want to get together with your substitute teacher or other teachers in your department and do your planning together. That will save even more time because you can help each other and share resources.

Knowing which lessons are coming up will get your brain attuned to those themes. Then as you go about your daily work, you will notice illustrations, materials, books, and other resources that you can plug into your lessons.

Planning gives you the big picture. Too many teachers are guilty of preparing "cake mix lessons." They have no idea how the curriculum is set up or what the quarter aims are. They simply mix up a lesson each Sunday and serve it ala carte instead of making it part of a quarterly banquet.

Planning provides balance. Knowing your needs in advance will keep you from neglecting important themes and needs of your class. It will help give a balance to your classes, because you will be able to see patterns or trends in your teaching style that need to be changed or improved.

Once my wife politely suggested that my lessons were getting "too psychological." She added, "You need to stick with the Bible." She was right; I had not noticed the drift in my lessons. Planning the lessons more carefully would have kept me from getting off onto a hobby.

How to Plan a Quarter's Lessons

I would recommend that you buy a sheet of poster board and divide it into thirteen vertical sections to correspond with the thirteen lessons in a quarter. Then fill in the chart with a summary of the lessons and some preliminary ideas and planning notes. A sample is included here in the text to give you an idea. After filling in the blanks of this chart, look it over carefully and ask yourself the following questions:

1. Have I scheduled everything that must be covered this quarter? Have I allowed for all interruptions, special events, and holidays?

2. Is my plan balanced? Am I using the same method too often? Did I give any assignments to students? If so, did I remember to check back on them?

3. Are there resources I could plug into this plan right now? Books I've read? Articles? A popular video or audio tape? A visiting missionary?

You may have to modify this chart to suit your age group and local needs. I would recommend you not spend a lot of time trying to make the poster into some kind of artwork. That takes time better spent in other ways.

When you are finished with your visual plan, post it on a wall where you will see it often—on the kitchen wall, by the door, above your desk. The more often you glance at this chart, the more your subconscious mind will work for you, reminding you of upcoming themes and giving you ideas 'out of the blue.'

Once you have an overview of the quarter, begin to concentrate on the first lesson that's upcoming. Don't allow your mind to be intimidated by all the other lessons to follow. Remember, you have only one lesson to prepare at a time.

Putting a Lesson Together

Recommending a procedure for lesson preparation is like recommending a brand of deodorant. What works for one person doesn't necessarily work for another. Nevertheless, here are some general ideas on preparing a lesson, in case you have never done it before. In time you will work out your own system.

Begin. Now is not the time to remodel your study, repair your computer printer, sharpen your pencils, or shop for a new chair. Don't prepare to prepare. Just begin, wherever you are, with whatever tools you have.

The sooner in the week that you begin, the more your subconscious mind will work for you throughout the week, and the less likely you are to panic at the last minute. Many good teachers begin on Sunday afternoon preparing their lesson for the next Sunday.

Book It. The mind needs information in order to create. After praying for God's guidance, begin by reading your lesson quarterly, including the "extras" such as the devotional texts, workbook, and take-home papers.

If any of the material is hazy to you, find a Bible commentary or dictionary and do some more reading. Your minister or bookstore can provide you with these tools. Don't stop reading until you have a good grasp of the lesson material and until it begins to speak to you personally. You'll know you are ready for the next step when you find yourself saying, "You know, this is good stuff! I can't wait to teach this!"

Breathe. Now that your mind is full of your lesson, put it aside for a while and let the information jell in your mind.

Brainstorm. Sometime in the middle of the week, or even sooner, sit down with a friend (husband, wife, teenage daughter, another teacher) and begin to rough in some ideas for how to teach this lesson. The methods section of this book will give you many starter ideas.

Spring Quarter

Date/Title	Text	Summary
March 7 "God's Generosity"	Matthew 20:1-16	Laborers in the vineyard
March 14 "Priorities"	Matthew 22:15-22	Jesus is questioned about taxes
March 21	NO CLASS	College Team Visiting
March 28 "Be Ready"	Matthew 25:1-13	The ten virgins and the wedding
April 4 "The Last Supper"	Matthew 26:17-35	New meaning to the Passover
April 11 "The Crucifixion"	Matthew 27:32-56	Tortures and meaning of the cross
April 18 (Easter) "Sorrow to Joy"	Matthew 28:1-20	How grief changes with the Good News

Ideas/Methods	Special Emphasis	Assignments/Quizzes
Grapes, pennies Role play it Review the quarter	Bulletin board preview of quarter's lessons	Pretest?
Guest lecture by IRS secretary who is class member	Make giant IRS Form 1040 for bulletin board	
ADULT CLASSES COMBINED		
Sing: "Give Me Oil in My Lamp"	Bulletin board display of wedding pictures	Meet with substitute teacher to plan next week's lesson
SUBSTITUTE TEACHER		
Ask nurses in class to tell about pain	Bulletin board: hammer and nails	Meet with substitute teacher for evaluation
SHORTENED CLASS PERIOD (Due to Easter drama)		Report on absentees

Don't worry about spit-and-polish at this stage. Just fire out some wild and crazy ideas that would be neat to try, and discuss them with your partner. Write them down on paper so you will have them when you need them.

After your brainstorm, make a list of materials you think you will need. Throughout the week you can collect these as you have time.

Blueprint. By now you should have a good grasp of your lesson and some gut feelings about what you want to accomplish. At this point, you need to get your plans down on paper in an orderly way. The next chapter of this book will describe a good, proven plan that you can follow.

Bear Down. It's Friday, or maybe even Saturday. You've been thinking, praying, playing around with some ideas. Now it's time to deliver this baby. Time to finalize your notes. Cut out your visuals. Prepare a bulletin board display. Drop by the church and check your classroom for cleanliness, adequate seating, and supplies. (The teens may have used it for a lock-in and it may be strewn with pizza boxes or gum wrappers.)

The more you do today to finalize your lesson, the less anxiety and confusion you will experience come Sunday morning.

Teach Your Lesson

No matter how well you have prepared, your class will never go exactly the way you planned it. That's because people are too complex to be manipulated like blocks or toy soldiers. Some of the things you planned will not work so well. Some things you never planned will work pretty good. When you are done, you will probably feel like both a success and a failure. That's normal. Teaching is something like playing baseball—some days you get to first base, some days you get to third base, and some days you hit a home run. Then again, once in a while you get beaned. Don't let any one class session discourage you from teaching. It takes time to learn, and even the best teachers have days when they strike out.

After each class session, take a little time to think over the lesson. Remember your successes, so you can try them again. Think about your fizzles and what you can learn from them. No class is ever a total failure, not for you and not for your students. Leave the results to God.

You've been given an overview of how to plan a quarter's

lessons and an overview of the process of lesson preparation. Now a few words about the curriculum itself.

The Curriculum

The term "curriculum" comes from a word for a racetrack and implies that teaching should follow a planned course of study to meet specific goals or objectives.

It may be that you, a teacher, will have little or no say in the content of your lessons. A church curriculum committee consisting of elders, the education minister, parents, and teachers may decide this matter for you, and that's probably wise. It's not a decision to be made lightly, nor should individual teachers be free to teach anything they wish. That kind of freedom is an open door to false doctrine and hobbyhorse themes.

Most churches will use a commercial curriculum from one of the major religious publishing house, such as Standard Publishing Company. These courses of study are written by professional writers and theologians who are qualified to put together a sound and progressive course of teachings.

Even so, no curriculum writer can design a perfect course that fits all your local church needs. That's why a curriculum committee takes the time to review several publishers' materials and then selects those materials that best suit local needs and objectives.

As a teacher you need to understand the makeup of the major curricula and how a curriculum is selected for your Sunday school. That way you can better reach the goals of the Sunday school.

If you are not happy with the materials you are teaching, perhaps you should approach the curriculum committee with your objections or offer to serve on the committee in the future.

Here are some of the things a curriculum committee looks for in a course of study.

1. Is the literature true to the Bible? It's difficult to find any commercial curriculum that agrees with all our personal opinions and judgments and which is one hundred percent doctrinally sound, as you might see it. Only the Bible itself is absolutely true-to-the-Bible. But a curriculum should be as close as humanly possible to the clear meaning of the Scriptures.

2. The New Testament should be emphasized in a curriculum, because that is the part of the Bible that has special rele-

vance to us in these end times. Although the course may include much from the Old Testament, it should include more texts from the New Testament. The Old Testament passages should be those that illustrate and emphasize New Testament truths.

3. The curriculum should prepare students in advance for the choices they will meet in life. It should cover those passages of text that help youth face the temptations and decisions that might otherwise overwhelm them. For example, a teenager should have enough Bible principles in mind that he is able to make wise decisions about sex, drinking, and career options.

4. A good curriculum should respect age differences and needs. For example, beginners need basic Bible vocabulary and concepts, whereas adults need material that helps them cope with the stresses of leadership roles. A graded curriculum does this. (See page ___ for a description of graded curriculum.)

5. A good curriculum will give some attention to contemporary problems such as drugs and gambling. But a curriculum that deals only with trendy subjects can inadvertently crowd out study of Bible principles.

Indeed, learning such principles as the body as a temple of the Spirit and stewardship may be the best kind of preparation for meeting contemporary problems like drugs and gambling.

6. Quality curriculum will include lessons that show respect for seasonal interests such as Christmas and New Year, when people's minds are already on these emotional topics. And a curriculum should have a certain amount of repetition built into it to reinforce important themes and to acquaint Sunday school newcomers with basic truths.

The Teacher as Curriculum

No matter what materials your church uses, the teachers themselves always determine how subjects are presented. In a real sense, the teacher himself is a major part of the curriculum by his character and emphasis of truth.

Curriculum materials are important, but they are not a messiah, nor are they a substitute for trained and educated teachers.

A good teacher can take average curriculum materials and produce outstanding lessons, and a so-so teacher can take outstanding materials and only come up with ho-hum classes.

Common Curriculum Approaches

Here is an overview of the more common types of curricula in use.

Through-the-Bible

At first glance this approach seems sensible and foolproof. And there are some through-the-Bible curricula that do a fair job with this approach.

But there are problems.

For one thing, the Bible is not assembled in strict chronological order. Events quickly become confusing unless the teacher is skilled with a time line or uses a chronological Bible.

Second, the Old Testament makes for a long, long study—fifty chapters in Genesis, sixty-six in Isaiah, one hundred fifty psalms. Start your course in Genesis, and you might still be in Genesis in the year 2095 A.D. Starting a study with Genesis will inevitably neglect the New Testament, which is the very part of the Bible that needs the most emphasis.

Starting at Matthew and going through the four Gospels can be equally confusing, like the little boy who thought that Jesus had been crucified four times, because the teacher had gone through the four Gospels consecutively.

Another form of the through-the-Bible curricula is the through-a-book approach. Usually a book of the Bible is selected by popular vote of the class or arbitrarily picked by the teacher because it's his favorite. The problem with this approach is that certain books of the Bible are universal favorites such as Genesis and James, and other books like Obadiah and Jude may get left out altogether. And if no one is keeping track of which books have been covered, a new teacher may end up teaching a book that was already taught by the former teacher.

If your Sunday school uses a through-the-Bible approach, select the most important passages from each book and occasionally alternate from Old Testament to New Testament for balance.

Uniform Lessons

For more than a century, the Uniform or single-theme lesson materials have been popular with Sunday schools in America and for good reasons.

The Uniform Lessons cover both Old and New Testaments, but include more lessons from the New Testament. Furthermore, the lessons go through a cycle every few years, and this provides the vital repetition of important themes. Few of us get things straight the first time around.

When all classes are studying the same theme or text, then dinnertime conversation over the lesson is possible and enjoyable. And if you are on vacation, you are likely not to miss your regular lesson when you visit another church, if they are using the Uniform Series.

The Uniform Lessons have been criticized because they seem to skip around. One Sunday you are studying from Jeremiah, and the next Sunday you are studying from Romans. But this is the very genius of the series, for it keeps a varied and balanced diet of Scriptures on your plate and does not let the teacher or students linger too long on a particular pet theme.

When several classes are using Uniform Lessons, teachers can get together and plan lessons and share materials, and there is usually an abundance of supplementary materials to go with Uniform Lessons.

Graded Lessons

Graded materials are best suited to the younger age groups where age differences are great. For example, Primaries are just learning to read and Young Teens are beginning to develop sexual characteristics. A lesson on love would have to be written one way for Primaries and another way for Young Teens.

In graded lessons, each department is presented with text selections and topics that are best suited to that age group. Primaries would be bored by a lesson on the genealogies, and teenagers wouldn't be interested in a lesson on aging from Ecclesiastes 12.

Graded lessons can cover the entire Bible or allow the teacher to emphasize passages most needed by his particular class of students.

Graded lessons are less popular with adults because all adults should be capable of studying any part of the Bible at any time.

Electives

In recent years, electives have become quite popular in many Sunday schools. This is both a blessing and a problem. Electives permit students and teachers to decide for themselves what topics or texts they want to study. Letting students decide for themselves is highly motivational because we tend to like what we get to choose for ourselves. In addition, the elective approach permits a teacher to insert a series of topics for which he is especially qualified to teach. For example, a Sunday school teacher who is a corporate president might be good with a series on leadership. And the elective approach allows students to plug into contemporary themes like abortion and the economy while they are hot topics.

A wide variety of elective studies is available, more all the time. There are workbooks, textbooks, videotapes, and visuals of all sorts on a great number of themes, from women's role in the church to Christian parenting.

However, the very popularity of electives can be a problem. Students and teachers alike can get so addicted to contemporary issues that the Bible itself is actually neglected. Students may fail to get familiar with Bible doctrines, terms, and structure. Indeed, a study of basic Bible truths may be the best preparation of all for meeting contemporary topics. It's tragic when a middle-aged man or woman has been in the Sunday school for years and is not familiar with basic Bible concepts because of a steady diet of electives.

Hybrid Approach

With so many different ideas about curriculum matters, what should a Sunday school do?

Graded lessons are a good bet for children, where needs are so precise and unique.

Teens and young adults are probably ready for electives and through-the-Bible.

Some churches solve the problem by offering a graded or Uniform curriculum for basic classes, with special elective classes for those who are well-grounded in the basics.

Your Part in the Curriculum

A good teacher will want to examine the curriculum materials he is using to get the big picture. Most commercial literature comes with a sampler or scope-and-sequence chart that shows how each lesson fits the overall plan. Ask your minister of education or publisher for this chart and get familiar with it. Some printed quarterlies show the entire series layout in the front cover or back cover.

Saying the Wrong

My Greatest Fear and Wors

One of my greatest fears as a teacher is that I will someday say something that is not true. I can't know everything, after all. Inevitably I will one day blurt out something like, "So then, Jesus rose from the grave on the fifth day." My junior high boys and girls will nod, trustingly.

Suddenly the sky grows dark, and the room begins to quake. Daggers of lightning explode through the window, missing me by millimeters. At the same time a trapdoor under me flies open, and I drop like a rock to a cold, damp holding cell.

I lie there in pitch darkness until the cell door opens and twelve grizzly elders march in and surround me. Beaming a bright light in my eyes, they grill me in basic Bible facts.

"Confess! Confess!" they chant. They pummel me with old quarterlies, but I can't remember what I said wrong.

Released, I stagger out of the cell, and crowds attack me, shouting, "Liar, liar, pants on fire, hangin' on a telephone wire!"

Nightmare

I race for home. Outrunning the mob, I lock myself in the house. I dig out all my books and comb the commentaries for some clue to my blunder.

The phone begins to ring off the wall.

"Hello, is this that guy who calls himself a teacher but doesn't know diddly? Well, get a job cleaning sewers and give these kids a break."

"Hello, I'm with the MacWrong Computer Systems, and I'd like to demonstrate our new classroom model that automatically corrects everything you teach. It's a steal this month at $9,000. . . ."

"Hello, this is Bobby Brat's dad, and I just wanna know if you've ever read that Scripture about somebody who offends the little ones and gets a millstone necklace and a free trip to clam country?"

"Hello, this the Fine Grind Millstone Company in Sandbucket, Montana. You have just won a lifetime supply of millstones. Where do you want this stone delivered?"

I feed the phone to the trash compactor and collapse on the couch to rest, but when I flip on the TV, Tom Brokaw is saying, "Tragedy today in a midwestern Sunday school, where more than a dozen innocent boys and girls were deceived by a vicious misinformationist masquerading as a Sunday school teacher. It was not a pretty sight. We go now to Missouri, where the victims are recuperating at a deprogramming center."

Overcome with remorse, I race back to the church building to see if I can recreate the scene of my crime and figure out what I said wrong. But the classroom is chained and locked, and guarded by a dozen armed goons.

Crimson with shame, I slink away to the local courthouse to have my name changed to "Anonymous." Then I board a plane to Sandbucket, Montana, to get a job in the Fine Grind Mines.

Now that you know what can happen when you make a mistake, here are some things to remember when it happens to you.

1. Only God never makes mistakes. The best teachers make mistakes, and usually no one even notices.

2. The one student who does catch your mistake will be sure to tell you about it, probably for a long time to come.

3. Your students share the responsibility for truth. They ought to test all things by the Word of God.

4. You aren't the only teacher they will ever have. Others may correct false impressions you have created.

5. If you are unsure of your facts, have someone knowledgeable check them in advance.

6. If you make a truly serious mistake, ask God to forgive it. He's good at that kind of thing.

7. There is no Sandbucket, Montana.

Chapter 5

The Lesson Plan

I love it when a plan comes together.
—Hannibal of the A-Team

"NOW HERE'S THE PLAN," my wife says whenever we are getting ready for a remodeling project or a trip. She's so good at planning. I'm quite sure the Lord is going to hire her to organize Judgment Day. She could do it!

Things seldom go exactly as planned, but without planning most projects are disabled at the start. When it comes to teaching, the same thing is true. Either I plan the lesson, or my students have a plan for the time.

The lesson plan provided in this chapter is flexible. It is not intended to suffocate you, but to serve you. Use it as a tool to meet the needs of your learners. Don't let it become a ball and chain.

Planning Potential

Here's a quick little quiz. What's the most important thing a teacher should do in planning a lesson?

❑ 1.   Read the quarterly.
❑ 2.   Take a nap.
❑ 3.   Sharpen pencils.
❑ 4.   Pray.
❑ 5.   Prepare visual aids.

If you answered "pray," then you win the teddy bear.

Why pray?

Because your class is God's class. He is the teacher, and you are his assistant. It's not all up to you, and you can't handle it by yourself. So pray. Pray for the lesson. Pray for students by name. Pray for wisdom.

This kind of heavenly contact will energize you and give you ideas. It will help you develop positive relationships with students and staff.

In training teachers, I have found that most young men and women trainees fall into one of two categories: the underconfident and the overconfident. Both extremes are dangerous, and prayer can help both types of personalities. I usually coach them something like this:

The underconfident: "Bring God into this lesson. He wants to help, and he will if you ask him. Do your part in preparation, and then ask his blessing. You can leave the results to him. The lesson may not go as you planned, but you can trust him to use it for good."

The overconfident: "God has given you much ability. You have a fine mind and a pleasing personality. Others probably envy your gifts. But God's blessing is more important than talent. Be certain to ask God for help with your lesson. Otherwise you may produce a lesson that is technically perfect but cold and sterile."

Know Your Learners

Of all Jesus' miraculous powers I suppose the one that fascinates me most is his ability to read minds. As John put it, "He did not need man's testimony about man, for he knew what was in a man" (John 2:25).

He knew the life history of the woman at the well.

He knew Simon Peter was about to fall before Simon knew it.

Unfortunately, my mind-reading powers are somewhat limited, and I suspect yours are too.

Not to worry. Even without miraculous powers you can do a lot to know your learners reasonably well. For example:

1. Familiarize yourself with the age group you are teaching. (See Chapter 3.) Most humans go through rather well-defined stages and have basically the same needs and desires at those times.

2. Build relationships with your students, using the telephone and the U.S. Mail to keep in touch throughout the week.

3. Observe your students and listen carefully to them. They are telling on themselves all the time. The student who hugs you constantly is showing his social hunger. The student who yawns all hour is in need of a challenge (or a good night's sleep). The student who bites his nails needs reassurance.

4. Hang around. Visit students at school; go to their ball games and concerts. "Puppies come to people who like puppies," is an old saying that applies to teaching and students. Show interest in students, and they will trust you with their affections and thoughts.

Begin With Scripture

Early in the week, teachers need to get acquainted with the Scripture text. How?

- Read it aloud to yourself.
- Read it into a cassette recorder, and play it on the car stereo as you drive.
- Write it on a large sheet of paper, and post it on a wall.

Let the text work on you throughout the week; then you will be better qualified to make it work in the lives of your students.

Take Aim

Robert Louis Stevenson once said something like, "A good aim is our chief need in life." He could have said the same thing about teaching, for aims are utterly indispensable to good teaching.

That's why curriculum writers provide unit and lesson aims in the quarterly. They give you a sense of direction. These aims are written true to the text and in line with the needs of each age group.

However, since the lesson writer has never met your students, you may have to slightly revise these aims for your specific needs.

Three kinds of aims are important.

Know

One kind of aim expresses what students should KNOW by the end of the lesson. This is sometimes thought of as an aim for the head. It is simply a statement of knowledge that is learned. For example:

1. Students will describe how God provided food for the Israelites in the wilderness.
2. Students will identify at least seven ways the man or woman of God is or acts opposite to a person of the world.

Feel

When students gain knowledge, they also begin to develop attitudes or feelings about that knowledge. Examples of FEEL aims are:

1. Students will feel confident that God will meet their needs.
2. Students will have a renewed commitment to the true joy and the proper behavior that should characterize a child of God.

This type of aim is almost impossible for the teacher to measure. Even so, it is important to keep in mind that most of us respond to knowledge when we have an attitude or feeling about it.

Do

The ultimate test of our teaching is the action or DO aim. The DO aim is sometimes thought of as the hands and feet aim. As a result of a feeling or attitude about information we know, we take action. For example:

1. Students will thank God for meeting their needs.
2. Students will demonstrate joy in at least two acts of kindness and mercy this week.

Not all aims are achieved by all learners and there is no specific time during a lesson when aims will be met. However, there are usually activities intended to lead to each aim.

Focusing on the aims in your teaching plan is really quite simple. Start with Scripture. Read and pray about the aims in the curriculum in light of what you know about the needs of your learners. Think about the relationship of the three kinds of aims. The KNOW aim states the information that will be learned. The FEEL aim helps to identify a feeling or attitude about the information and leads the learner to the DO or action aim. The FEEL aim is a bridge between the KNOW and DO aims.

Understanding and using aims insures meaningful learning and changed lives.

The Learning Session

There are three essential parts to a good learning session.

Readiness Activities

Learners are seldom "with it" at the start of class. Activities in this section are geared to getting learners' attention and building appetite for the Bible study. Typical activities include a game, singing, a pretest, a story, or a craft related to the lesson theme.

Bible Study Activities

When the attention of learners is focused, you are ready for activities that communicate and reinforce the lesson text.

Adults

KNOW: Pupils will know what makes a good prayer.
FEEL: Pupils will feel the need to pray.
DO: Pupils will be able to verbalize a prayer.

READINESS: Discussion—Our failures in prayer life.
(10 minutes)   List—Wishes for a better prayer life.

BIBLE STUDY: Lecture—Elements of prayer from Matthew 6:9-13 (confession,
(30 minutes)   adoration, thanksgiving, etc.).
                 Bible prayer search—Great prayers in the Bible (i.e., Job,
                    Moses, Abraham, Hannah, Mary).
                 Hymn prayers—Sing or read some prayer hymns and discuss
                    what makes them good (honesty, clarity, brevity, etc.).

APPLICATION: Brainstorm—Things to pray about besides just sickness.
(20 minutes)   Writing—Each student writes a short prayer and reads it aloud.
                 Prayer—Prayer circle.

Youth

KNOW: Pupils will know what makes a good prayer.
FEEL: Pupils will feel the need to pray.
DO: Pupils will be able to verbalize a prayer.

READINESS: Buzz group—"What are some of the worst prayers you have
(15 minutes)   ever heard?" (repetitious, vague, long, etc.).

BIBLE STUDY: Bible prayer search—Young people who prayed in the
(25 minutes)   Bible (i.e., Samuel, Joseph, David, Solomon) and the results
                  of their prayers.
                 Analogy discussion—How is prayer like/unlike talking to your
                    girl/guy on the phone? How is prayer like accessing informa-
                    tion on your computer? How is prayer like asking your father
                    for the car keys?

APPLICATION: Poster creation—Divide into groups to write and illustrate
(20 minutes)   prayers on a given theme.
                 Recording studio—Read the prayers into a cassette recorder.
                 Discuss how you would answer them, not answer, etc.
                 Prayer—One phrase prayers.

Elementary Age Children

KNOW: Pupils will know that Paul continued to tell the good news even when discouraging things happened.

FEEL: Pupils will feel sad for missionaries who feel discouraged.

DO: Pupils will encourage and pray for a missionary to keep telling the good news.

READINESS:
(20 minutes)

Cassette tape—Play tape of discouraged people. Think of ways to encourage them.

Song-writing—Read Acts 18:1-11. Summarize the story by writing words to a familiar tune.

BIBLE STUDY:
(20 minutes)

Discussion—Have you ever felt discouraged? What encourages you?

Storytelling

Singing—Pupils sing their story songs.

APPLICATION:
(20 minutes)

Activity book—"What would you say to encourage these people?"

Letter-writing—Write an encouraging letter to a missionary.

Prayer—Pray for missionaries. Each pupil will use the sentence, "Help ____ be encouraged to speak about Jesus when ____."

Preschool Age Children

KNOW: Pupils will identify ways God cared for David and/or helped him be brave.

FEEL: Pupils will feel secure in God's help and care.

DO: Pupils will thank God for his care.

READINESS:
(25 minutes)

Art Center—Make a nine-foot silhouette of Goliath.

Music Center—Use rhythm instruments and cassette tape to talk about how David thanked God with his songs.

Quiet Center—Puzzles about David and puzzles about prayer.

BIBLE STUDY:
(15 minutes)

Storytelling—Flannelgraph of David and Goliath.

APPLICATION:
(20 minutes)

Pictures—Talk about what to do when we are afraid.

Finger play—"God Is Bigger Than Goliath."

Activity book—Color/sticker page.

Prayer—Children repeat prayer phrases after the teacher.

Activities might include research, small group discussion, or Bible story time. Activities should be age related, and a variety should be used. Consult your curriculum for specific suggestions. Consider the interests, needs, and abilities of your learners.

Application Activities

During this part of the session, students are urged to make plans to carry into life what they have learned in the hour. For example, a student may develop a personal plan to witness to a friend after observing a role play.

Applications are a very personal thing. A teacher can only guide students. Students cannot be forced to obey. But practical suggestions and discussion can help extend the lesson beyond the four walls of your classroom.

Chapter 6

Mastering Methods

The best method is the right method.
The worst method is any method you overuse.

TOOLS ARE WONDERFUL things. Oh, they aren't always much to look at. There's not much glamour in a monkey wrench or a crowbar. No one is going to display a claw hammer in the Smithsonian or decorate a banquet table with a crosscut saw. But tools are able to create beautiful things: fine cabinets, sleek cars, fragrant flower gardens.

Tools are so special that many mechanics and carpenters get attached to them as though they were children. They prize them and care for them as if they were crown jewels.

Tools enable workers to do things that they couldn't do with their bare hands or by brute force. I once did a valve job on a 57 Dodge. It took me a week to insert the valve keepers by hand. Then my father handed me a tool that would do the job in minutes. Embarrassing!

Methods are a teacher's tools, and the more a teacher understands his tools the more beauty he will be able to produce in his students.

Some teachers have only one tool in their tool kit—the lecture method. No matter what the text, the class, the subject, they always lecture. It's possible to drive nails with a screwdriver instead of a hammer, but it's not easy. And it's possible to teach students to do a craft using the lecture method, but it's a lot easier with a demonstration or a model along with class participation.

91

In this chapter we are going to look at some of the tools that should be in a teacher's tool kit. Beginning teachers will need time to learn each method, so be patient with yourself if you are just starting out. You don't learn to use a power saw in one day, so don't expect to master methods too quickly. Stay with a method until it begins to work for you. Then try another method until you master it too.

Overview

First, look over this listing of methods that is particularly suited to specific age groups. Check the age group you will be teaching. In the pages that follow we will look at several of the "big" methods, the "meat and potatoes" of teaching. Most new methods and many minor methods are really just variations of these major methods of teaching. If you are familiar with the "big" ones, you will be able to adapt to new methods as they come along.

The Big Decision

With so many methods available, how does a teacher decide what to use and when? Here are some things to consider in making the choice.

1. Select more than one method. Seldom will one method work for an entire hour, especially one like lecture that is heavy, and allowing no participation. Using three different methods in an hour is a good rule of thumb.

2. How much time do you have for teaching? Methods such as class projects and discussion take an inordinate amount of time to set up and execute.

3. How many pupils are there in your class? The more pupils, the slower things will go, as a rule. If you have a super large class (100-300), you may be confined to lecture with visuals, panel discussions, and so forth. If you have a very small class (3-6 pupils), you could easily handle projects and learning centers.

4. How is your classroom equipped? If you can't darken the room, it may be hard to use projected visuals. If the chairs can't be moved around, then discussions may be difficult.

5. What are your skills? Some teachers try lecture, but are so insecure that they soon quit from frustration. Other teachers try to lead discussion and find that they can't get anyone to talk.

Age-Specific Teaching Methods

Toddler-Kindergarten (1-5 years)

conversation	toy play	show and tell	short memory verses
music/singing	workbooks	puppets	rhythm/rhyme
verbal praise	pictures	games/puzzles	reading aloud
rest time	marching	taking offering	vocabulary
refreshments	crafts	finger plays	storytelling
prayer			

Primary-Middler (6-9 years)

social play	pictures	crafts	workbooks
computer play	flannelgraph	singing/music	conversation
simple group drama	displays	reading aloud	puppets
creative writing	humor	audio/video tapes (participatory)	
learning centers	worship	games (non-competitive)	
prayer			

Juniors (10-11 years)

memory work	audio tapes	Bible drills	map work
chalkboard work	competition	short projects	creative writing
construction projects	puppets	computers	learning centers
crafts/art activities	workbooks	short lecture	games
murals/graffiti boards	chronology work	short discussion	parties
question and answer	assignments	video tapes	field trips

Teens (12-17 years)

short student reports	debates	parties/lock-ins	short lecture
group discussions	handouts	making videos	drama
making transparencies	class projects	brainstorming	short interviews
magazine searches	panel discussions	art activities	question and answer
making slide shows	fun tests	TV quiz shows	

Adults

lecture	student reports	class meetings	case studies
panel discussions	slides and videos	transparencies	overhead
question and answer	study teams	brainstorming/mind-mapping	
choral readings	visiting speakers	large group discussions	
tests/questionnaires		small group discussions	

This chart is merely suggestive, not a legal document. Some teachers have found real creative success by using methods not "usually" used with their age-group. For example, one adult teacher uses a flannel board with great success in his young adult class. Another teacher uses a panel discussion with Primaries.

What are your strengths? How can you use them in your classroom?

6.   What is the text and your aim? Some lesson texts automatically lend themselves to certain methods. Bible stories make good dramas. The book of Job makes for good discussion. The psalms lead naturally into worship activities.

Lecture Method

A lecturer is someone who talks in your sleep.
  I hear, and I forget.
  Telling is not teaching, and listening is not learning.
  I could listen to him speak for hours at a time.

In recent years the lecture method has received some bad press. As other methods became popular, some teachers began to abandon the lecture altogether.

That is a mistake.

The lecture method is as valid as ever. It's only bad lectures that are inappropriate, or constant lecture, which is tedious. A good lecture is a thing of beauty. An uninterrupted speech allows a teacher to cover much material quickly and to add his enthusiasm and energy to the material. And the lecture method lets students watch their teacher at work with language and communication skills—skills they need to see modeled.

Furthermore, in lectures a teacher does the research for his class, thus saving them study time and saving himself class time. By lecturing, the teacher can present materials that his students could not find anywhere else.

Alas, not every teacher is good at lecture, and some age groups simply won't sit still for a lengthy lecture. Even so, lectures are useful and often can be improved with a little effort.

Lecture Tips

To be a better lecturer, consider the following suggestions:

1.   Deliver thick and chewy. Make sure your lecture has enough juicy information to make it interesting and informative. One kernel of wheat in a bushel of sawdust will not make a good talk.

2.   Keep it fresh. Last year's notes probably will not make a good lecture this year unless you freshen them up. Illustrations get dated quickly. Statistics change. Language changes. Sometimes it's best just to start over with fresh material.

3. Remember the plus factor. No matter what the theme of your lectures, be sure to make them upbeat. Students are already ladened with problems. They come to Sunday school to find support, not a kick in the face. True, a teacher has to deal with negative subjects, and he has to rebuke sin. That's all right as long as the teacher puts Humpty Dumpty back together again before the class is over. Give your students hope. It's a constant and deep need of humans.

Lecture Styles

There's more than one way to lecture, and a good teacher will occasionally vary the style of his presentations. Here are some alternative approaches to the straight lecture.

Programmed Lecture Instead of speaking nonstop for an hour, break your lecture up into five- or ten-minute segments. It's hard to drink from a fire hose, and it's hard for students to take in a relentless lecture. In between each five-minute segment, ask the class a question over the previous material, or insert something entirely different in the spaces between lecture—something like a joke or a story. This approach will better suit younger age groups whose attention span is short. It will keep you, the teacher, from getting carried away with your own eloquence until you sound more like an auctioneer than a teacher. When students see that you are going to ask them a question now and then, they will be listening with intent.

Shared Lecture The trouble with most lectures is that students have to listen to the same monotonous voice all hour. Consider bringing an assistant to class to help you with your lecture. It could be your wife or husband, your son, or a friend. Give the assistant part of the lecture to present, even if it's just a story or a list of statistics to read. Having a different voice will break the boredom. If you are teaching older teens through adults, consider giving students portions of your lecture to present at certain times. Before class, give them the poem, Scripture, or story you want them to present, so they will have time to bone up on it before class begins.

Worksheet Lecture If you've ever tried to take notes on a lecture, you know that it's sometimes difficult to keep up with the speaker. You can get so caught up in taking notes that you don't have time to think about what the speaker is saying. Solution? Provide students with a handout that lists your main points with spaces provided for them to write in minor points and quotes. This will give them some mental space to enable them to digest what you are saying. Plus, it encourages all students to take notes. Yes, it will cost a bit of time and money to make the handout, but it will raise the value of your teaching a great deal.

Visual Lecture Most lectures could be improved immensely by merely adding a visual touch. It doesn't have to be something elaborate or costly. Just pause and put a few words on the chalkboard. Show a couple slides. Hold up a poster. Use a sketch pad and stick figures, or numbers, or symbols. Pass around a picture in a book. Play a bit of a popular song. Do a short mime or role play. Use some flash cards. Pass around a newspaper clipping.

Directed Lecture Instead of just droning on and on, direct each row of your class to listen for certain things in your lecture. Then debrief them when you are done. Ask one row to listen for statistics, another row to listen for the general meaning, and a third row to listen for illustrations. Halfway through the lecture, pause and ask them what they saw and heard. This type of lecture is based on the fact that *if you don't know what you are looking for, you won't find it*. By directing their purpose for listening, you help them find specific things in the lecture.

The Red Flags

As powerful as a lecture can be, there are some dangers in it. The most obvious danger is its tendency to act as a sleeping tablet. One nervous college student played tapes of his most boring teacher to put himself to sleep at night!

Here are some other trouble spots.

1. Inadequate preparation. The teacher is one minute into his lecture when it becomes apparent that he doesn't have his material well in mind.

2. Trying to impress. The teacher's job is to express, not impress. Trying to be too cute or to dazzle students with a large vocabulary will be counterproductive.

3. Disregard for the audience. If your students are uncomfortably seated, the lighting poor, the acoustics terrible, and the room trashy—subtract ten from your presentation. Try to make your classroom an orderly, quiet place where a lecture can succeed without having to compete with other distractions.

4. Substitute for teaching. Don't forget that there are many good ways to teach. Don't let lecture become a chronic habit. Predictability is death in teaching. Variety is life.

Discussion Method

Talk is cheap . . . and worth its weight in gold.

The discussion method of teaching is probably the most "American" of all methods. It's a method that thrives in any free society, and a host of popular television talk shows attest to its strength.

Let's face it, it's fun to talk and to eavesdrop on others who are talking. That adds motivation to discussion classes. But it's also one of the better ways to reach the truth. Two heads are better than one when it comes to solving problems and finding answers. Discussions are persuasive too. The dynamics of a group are powerful motivators and change agents. "As iron sharpens iron," said Solomon, "so one man sharpens another" (Proverbs 27:17).

If you are teaching junior high through adult, then discussion method is a natural choice, especially when combined with a bit of lecture.

Discussion Styles

Actually, there are many different kinds of discussion. Here are a few.

Interviews Television has made the interview the standard method of getting information fast. Likewise, employers rely on interviews to get acquainted with prospective employees in a hurry. How can interviews be used in Sunday school?

Interview personalities such as visiting missionaries, the elderly, a member of Alcoholics Anonymous, teachers, boy scout leaders, doctors—anyone who might have some insight on the lesson at hand. Usually these people will be glad to visit your class and "have their brains picked."

Interview students. When it comes time to apply the lesson, divide your class into pairs. Give them a list of questions, and have them interview each other about how the lesson is relevant to their own needs. To review a lesson, give questions to each pair, and let them interview each other.

Get acquainted with visitors in your class. Take a few moments to interview them in front of the class to help make them welcome.

Interview counterparts. When teaching a lesson on Simon Peter, the fisherman, interview a modern-day fisherman. When talking about Cornelius, the soldier, interview someone in the armed forces. Ask questions that help your students see the lesson truths in modern terms.

Buzzes Buzz groups are an old standby method of letting students get into the act.

1.   Neighbor Nudge: Because most regular students tend to sit by a friend, a quick way to get discussion is to ask your students to talk to their neighbor about a given topic. A chance to talk aloud to a neighbor is irresistible and productive.

2.   Blitz: Put your class into groups of no more than ten people and give each of them a topic to discuss. Set a time limit such as coming up with ten ideas in ten minutes. The time factor adds excitement.

3.   Four-On-The-Floor: Put young people in groups of four on the floor, and give them a series of fast-moving topics to discuss, changing the topic every so many minutes. Then put them back in rows and debrief them.

Buzz groups can be used at the beginning of the hour to get interest built up, as a mid-class break, or as an end of class application time. They work best when the teacher prepares students with a specific handout of questions or a topic.

Brainstorms and Mind-mapping If you are looking for ideas, lesson applications, or lists of examples, then brainstorming is a good way to go. Students can brainstorm as a class, or you can break them into groups for more efficiency. Urge them to make suggestions without prejudging. Work visually, writing their ideas on the chalkboard or poster board. About ten percent of the ideas they suggest will probably be worthwhile, but quantity and speed are important to finding that ten percent. You can enhance a brainstorm by offering small monetary awards for ideas or by putting students into competitive teams.

Mind-mapping is another way of brainstorming. Put the brainstorm ideas on the board. Then connect the ideas together and ask for new combinations or new ideas. For example, in brainstorming ways that class members can show love to their friends, you might get such answers as: hang around them, invite them to your home, send them notes, or give them gifts. In mind-mapping you might go further by combining these ideas to come up with: "send someone a gift with a note attached," or "invite the person to your home to receive a gift."

Panels Panel discussions offer the teacher a chance to tap the experts in his class. If teaching young adults, you might form a panel of husbands to talk about "What wives can do to make us more spiritual," or a panel of service workers to talk about "How we can put quality into our service to others."

The key to a good panel discussion is in having good quality questions that do not threaten, but do open students' minds.

Case Studies The daily newspaper contains enough emotional information to stimulate hours of discussion. If your class includes mature, informed students like middle-aged adults, then you might begin class by reading a news story and asking questions such as, "How likely is it that this would ever happen to any of us? What would you have done in the same situation? What is the moral thing to do? How would today's lesson help with this situation?"

This method has one danger. Sometimes it works too well, and it's difficult to get students back to the lesson text. You will have to get "tough" with them, and be sure not to neglect the Scriptures.

Discussion Secrets

A discussion is like a giant snowball. It's hard to get it moving, and then it's hard to control it when it does move.

How do you get a discussion rolling?

1. Use a discussion starter. Here are some types of starters.

Activities: For a lesson on the lost coin, hide a coin somewhere in the class and stage a quick treasure hunt. For a lesson on the blind man Jesus healed, blindfold all students and let them walk around bumping into things.

Guide sheets: Provide students with a stimulating handout that will get them into the subject—agree/disagree statements, prioritizing activities, or a listing of dogmatic statements or proverbs.

Audiovisuals: Show a portion of a video or filmstrip, or play a bit of an audio tape. Then give students a handout with questions that coordinate with the visual starter and the text.

2. The second key to good discussions is having good questions. What makes up a good discussion question? Several things. Good discussion questions are emotional, open-ended, and challenging. Here are some poor-good contrasts to show you the difference.

Poor: "What does Paul say we must endure as Christians?"
Good: "Of all the problems Paul endured, which would you find hardest to endure?"
Poor: "Where was Jesus born?"

Good: "If Jesus were born today in our town, how would his birth be different?"

Poor: "How can we better serve Christ?"

Good: "If I gave you one thousand dollars, how would you use it for Christ?"

Writing good questions is hard work, but really good questions are the single most important key to effective discussions.

3. Having a good topic is another way of ensuring good discussion. Where can you find surefire topics? Study the characteristics of your age group. (See Chapter 3.) For example, college ages are interested in careers and marriage. Read a few issues of magazines that your students read, or listen to some of the tapes they listen to. Universal human needs are always good too. People are almost always interested in some facet of universal themes like love, money, sex, guilt, hope, faith, time.

Most importantly, keep your ears open when you are around your students in the hallways or during recreational and social activities. They give clues as to their interests when they don't know anyone is listening.

The Red Flags

1. Discussion is not a savior, and its limits must be respected. Not everyone makes a good discussion leader. If you are a strong personality with authoritarian ways, then students may not discuss for you.

2. Discussion can also get out of control, leaving the lesson far behind. A guide sheet helps, but the teacher must sometimes take charge and prevent "wandering around in the wilderness of opinions."

3. The biggest disadvantage of discussion is that it takes so much time to do well. Don't use it when you are in a hurry to cover material.

Storytelling Method

Teacher, this lesson is awfully dull. Tell us a story!

There is probably no teaching method that can top the storytelling method. It's one of the oldest. It can be used with all age groups. It was a favorite of Jesus, and has become popular in recent times because of storytellers such as Bill Cosby, Paul

Harvey, and Garrison Keillor.

Storytelling makes complicated ideas simple enough for a child. It keeps people on the edge of their seats. It's good therapy. It tickles the imagination. It transcends time and space. It can be used with large groups or as an intimate medium with a child on your lap.

When all other methods of teaching fail, storytelling still works. It has been called "the only painless method of learning," and its power is awesome.

And there are so many kinds of stories: fables, parables, folk tales, legends, jokes, chain stories, myths, fairy tales, Bible stories, contemporary fiction, and many more.

The Secret of Storytelling

There is basically one key to effective storytelling, and it's simple. *Know the story!* Know the story so well that you love it and long to tell it. Know it so well that you don't falter or fumble when telling it. Know it so well that you are anxiety-free and able to put in sound effects and gestures and emotions. Some teachers can't tell stories because they really don't have a story to tell. Or they have a poor story that doesn't excite them or prove anything. But if a teacher has a good story, knows it well, and loves it from the heart, it's hard to fail. Leave its effect to the divine storyteller.

How do you get to know a story well? Start by reading it several times. Diagram the plot on a scrap of paper. Look up any unfamiliar words or terms. Visualize the setting in full color. Imagine the smells, sights, tastes, and touches of the characters and events. Check out places on a map. Explore little details in the story like names and weather and nouns.

And then practice.

And practice some more.

Finding Good Stories

Where do you find all these good stories? Start with the Bible, which is a fine collection of stories. *The Subject Guide to Bible Stories* (compiled by George Frederick Garland, Robert H. Sommer, Publisher, 1969) will help you find stories that match certain themes. Some encyclopedia series include a guide to selecting stories for every age group. Newspapers contain human interest stories. Magazines such as *Guideposts*, *Reader's Digest*, and *The Lookout* contain collections of stories. There are books of hymn stories available in Bible bookstores. Devotional books contain stories. Sermon books are loaded with stories as are elementary and high school readers. Inspirational books by Schuller, Peale, Mandino, and others contain motivational stories. Check anthologies and short-story collections. The children's and young adult libraries are rich sources of stories that can be used with both adults and children. Ask your librarian for the names of popular books and books with moral themes.

Telling the Tale

Every storyteller tells a story differently, but certain principles will help all teachers do a better job.

1. Choose a good story. A so-so story cannot be repaired by voice inflections or tricks.

2. Start slow and soft to allow yourself room to expand your volume and emphasis.

3. Vary your delivery. Insert pauses, sound effects, gestures and facial expressions freely. A "gimmick" sometimes helps—a flower in your hand for a nature story, a "story hat" to create a mood, or some background music to hide room and body noises.

4. Inexperienced storytellers may find it is easier to "read-tell" a book than to tell a story without notes. Find a storybook, and turn the pages and tell it rather than read it. If you get stuck, you can always read the text for a while.

5. Watch for interruptions in storytelling. Your train of thought can be shattered by latecomers or even by questions from your students during the story.

Variations on the Theme

Telling a story "straight" is probably the best way to tell stories, but there are many other ways of telling stories. Here are a few.

1. Use a series of objects or things to illustrate your words. For example, in telling the story of the pearl of great price, you could use a variety of jewelry and paper money. Then use a Ping-Pong ball for the pearl of great price. Having a series of objects helps you to remember the next line of your story.

2. Put your listeners into the story with a visual or gift. For example, in telling the story of Sodom and Gomorrah, one teacher gave each student some red-hot candies which she

"rained" on the cities to represent fire and brimstone. Another teacher served goldfish crackers for the story of the feeding of the five thousand.

3. Tell a continuing story. Each Sunday for six weeks, read or tell a portion of a story at the end of each lesson. Begin each week with a bit of review.

4. Open-ended stories are good for making students think. Tell an unfamiliar story right up to the end. Then let the class guess how it ends or decide how it should end for a Christian. Then read them the real ending. Or tell a portion of a story, then stop and discuss it. Then tell more of it and so forth.

5. If you are very shy, tell the story at home to your cassette recorder. Then play it to your class, using visuals to help keep their attention—a series of overhead transparencies or objects, for example.

6. Tell a participation story. Give students certain sounds or motions to do on cue in a story. Then tell the story, and let each student do his part.

The Red Flags

1. You're a teacher, not an entertainer. Use stories to *teach*.

2. Make sure students get the right *point* from your story, since most stories have several points.

3. Don't overuse stories and wear students out.

Drama Method

Sunday school is a stage, and the teachers are its actors.

Acting out the truths of the Scripture is a kind of "storytelling with skin." During drama, emotions run high and students tend to remember for a long time any moral truth they have acted out.

Kinds of Drama

Several categories of drama are useful in the Sunday school, and each one can be adapted to certain age groups.

Very young children can begin their drama acquaintance by posing a picture. Show the children a picture, perhaps of Jesus and the disciples in the boat during the storm. Put the children in a big cardboard box boat, and ask them to pose the scene while you tell the story.

Miming is for slightly older children who know how to imitate you. You do the mime of the Bible story, and your students mime or imitate you.

Young children can also do a form of role-playing if you are careful not to push them or embarrass them. For example, you can ask your entire class to stand and hold out their arms to be "trees" as you tell the story of Zacchaeus. You can use finger plays and simple puppets to let them tell the story in their own way. One simple way to acquaint children with drama is to provide them with a costume/prop box. Tell them a Bible story. Then let them use the costumes to review or retell the Bible story.

Teens are ready for real role play, simulation, or full-fledged drama.

A role play is a brief drama (2-3 minutes) of some Bible theme or story. Role play uses few or no props, and is followed by a discussion.

A simulation is a lengthy role play with reading parts and minor props, but not rehearsed. A drama is a full-scale production with props, memorized parts, and rehearsal.

Role plays, obviously, are the best bet for everyday classroom use, since they require less preparation and less execution time.

Here are some of the kinds of role plays that teachers find useful.

1. Bible events and stories are fairly easy to duplicate. Assign students certain character parts, and let them plan their own approach to the story. Prepare a set of discussion questions to go with the drama. Otherwise the role play may be just another game.

2. Morality dramas can be contemporary portrayals of Bible truth. For example, a lesson on the good Samaritan might lend itself to a role play about a bag lady.

3. How-to role plays are used for training, in the same way that a wedding rehearsal prepares everyone for the wedding. If you teach adults, you may want to role-play approaches to counseling someone, soul winning, ushering, or listening skills.

4. Novelty role plays would include puppet shows and humorous skits. You might teach teens what it's like to have your house vandalized by letting them draw or paint pictures. Then vandalize them while they are out of the room, and discuss how it feels. A charade is a type of role play that can be used for review. Let students guess which character the role players are simulating with the charade.

Making Drama Work

The trick in using drama is making it more than just entertainment. You want it to teach moral truth and not just entertain. How can you do that?

1. Prepare the audience to receive the role play. While the actors are out of the room preparing their skit, discuss with the class the principle that the actors are going to illustrate.

2. After the skit, talk about it. A written list of questions in handout form is helpful.

3. Some role plays can be replayed to make a different point. For example, have students role-play the wrong way to witness at school. Then reverse it, and have them role-play the right way to witness.

4. Follow the role play with a writing exercise. Have students write down what they think the characters were thinking and feeling. Then discuss these with the rest of the class.

The Red Flags

1. Like any method, role playing can be overused and it loses its appeal.

2. Very shy classes may resist role playing at first. You may have to do the first one yourself to set the example.

3. Role plays can get out of hand. Try not to typecast a person—it's too revealing and embarrassing. Don't let a role play run on too long.

4. Be warned that some churches are opposed to role play of any kind. They feel it smacks of theater, which they feel does not belong in the church. Some also are opposed because role playing is sometimes used in public schools to build sympathy for special interests such as homosexual life styles, unwed mothers, etc. In this case, their objection is really to the type of role play, not to role playing itself.

Role plays remain a valid instructional method, despite their criticisms and drawbacks.

Activity Method

Busy hands, busy hearts.

Many types of activities or projects are suitable for classroom use. Here are a few.

Learning Centers

Also known as interest centers and study stations, learning centers are areas of the room devoted to certain types of supervised work and play. Sometimes a teacher will set up the room with three or four centers, all of which the student is required to visit during the lesson hour. The teacher and an assistant visit with the children at these centers to make sure they learn what they are supposed to learn and to help keep order.

Learning centers are valuable because we tend to remember most of what we *do,* rather than what we hear. Teachers use them to teach new truth, to reinforce ideas, and to capture the interest of early arrivers. Many students like the freedom of a learning center—freedom of choice, freedom to move around, freedom to talk and ask questions. Learning centers allow a teacher to give individual students close attention.

Suppose you are teaching Psalm 23. You might set up a table-top learning center with things to observe, make, and do—pictures of sheep and shepherds, a sheep puppet to play with, a tape recording that tells what a shepherd's life is like, a set of questions about the psalm to be answered on paper or with a computer. Add sticks for making a shepherd's staff, and a list of other Bible passages on sheep to be looked up by students. The teacher might even dress up as a shepherd, and bring a real lamb to class.

A missions learning center might include a taped message from the missionary, pictures of the mission, a map to fill in points of interest, and some samples of foreign food such as french fried snails.

There are several good books for teachers that tell about learning centers and some commercially prepared learning centers available in bookstores.

Making the learning center more than just fun is accomplished by talking to students (including the Bible in your conversation), by having a theme to the center, and by posting and enforcing rules such as being courteous to others, working quietly, and following directions carefully.

Some of the more common types of learning centers for young children include: housekeeping center, book center, puzzle center, play dough center, science center, art center, and a Bible or worship center.

Learning centers are not trouble-free. For example, if you are the kind of teacher who simply can't endure watching children make mistakes, then it will be hard for you to be patient while students fumble at the centers. The centers take time—sometimes more time than you have to prepare or more class time than you can justify. Keeping everybody busy all the time is another problem, but teachers who really enjoy using learning centers can work out these bugs.

Quiz Shows

Many television shows can be staged in your class as a means of teaching or reviewing information. Shows like "Jeopardy!" and "Wheel of Fortune" can be imitated with lesson questions and truths.

For example, you could make an acetate spinner for your overhead projector to be your "wheel of fortune." Ask a girl volunteer to be Vanna White and keep score at the chalkboard. Divide your class in half and start the questions. Afterward, discuss faulty answers and related ideas.

Crafts

Most teachers of young children instinctively have a craft time to reinforce the lesson theme. It is especially important that it apply to the lesson, rather than just be something to do or take up time.

Some teachers prefer low-structure activities. They merely provide students with paper, scissors, glue, etc., and let them interpret the lesson in pictures, cutouts, and finger painting. Other teachers prefer to give students specific things to make and very specific instructions in how to do it.

Successful craft time requires several things:

- Planning. You must have adequate materials available, or you will soon have fighting and tears among students.
- Good instructions. Little hands get frustrated when they don't know how to make something. It also takes patience to demonstrate a craft and then to help individual students complete their projects.
- Motivation. Although most children like to make and do things, it is highly encouraging when the teacher posts their work on the bulletin board or sends it home to praising parents.
- Age-appropriate work. When students are asked to do things beyond their skills, they lose interest. When you give them

something that is "old hat," you may also find them in rebellion. Study the characteristics of each age group (see Chapter 3), and talk to public school teachers about appropriate crafts for each age group.

Art Activities

As students reach the teen years, they are more capable of producing art that is worthy of keeping. They are also good at group art activities and construction projects. Some of the more common ones include mural making, graffiti boards, collages, and montages.

One group of Young Teens made a room-size model of the wilderness tabernacle. They gave their parents guided tours of the model with explanations of all the parts and their meanings.

Other successful projects include: making a wooden bookcase of the books of the Bible, Bible time lines, painting the walls with Bible scenes, and even making Bible character costumes.

Making room decorations to fit the lesson theme is a common way of reinforcing the lesson. But this is usually best done before or after class to save teaching time.

Service Projects

More and more young people are becoming interested in "real" activities as a means of learning and growing. Perhaps this is a positive outcome of our activist age and the special-interest groups they observe on television. Most of these projects have to be done out of class, on the student's own time. But sometimes preparations for these projects can be done in class. For example, a class of third graders might make get-well cards in class, then go on a field trip to the nearby hospital to distribute the cards.

Some other popular projects include:

- Fixing up or cleaning a local Christian camp
- Environmental clean-up projects
- Writing to orphans at a Christian home, followed by a visit
- Making devotional booklets to take to nursing home
- Planting flower boxes for Sunday school windows
- Videotaping a choir to play at nursing homes
- Repairing and cleaning church hymnals

There are many books that suggest project ideas. Always try to relate the project to the Bible lesson for extra learning effect. For example, a lesson on the feeding of the five thousand would lead naturally into collecting food for the food kitchen.

The Red Flags

1. Projects tend to take more time and work than any other teaching method.

2. Sometimes it's hard to get some learners motivated, and they sometimes perform with the wrong motives.

3. The teacher is the key to making projects more than just busy work. It's the teacher's job to make each activity a teaching/learning experience.

The Round Robin,   The Talking Head,

After nine thousand years of educational research, Sunday school teachers still prefer three tried and true methods of teaching. Drop into a typical adult Sunday school class and you're likely to experience the Round Robin, the Talking Head, or the Hot-Air Forum.

The Round Robin

In this method the teacher begins class by saying, "Let's go around the room and have everybody read a verse of the text and the comments that go with it."

This sounds like a good idea. At least everyone will have a part of the lesson and no one person can hog the ball.

But there are problems. Whenever I'm in such a class and the teacher announces the Round Robin procedure, I immediately begin to count the number of students sitting in front of me so I can figure out which verse will be mine. That way I can practice pronouncing the big words.

"Let's see, would that be 'Cannonites' or 'Caneonites'?" I mutter to myself. "And what's this 'Jeshuran' anyway?"

Meanwhile I'm not hearing a word the teacher or other students are saying because I'm so worried about my own verse. As the turn taking gets closer and closer to me, I can feel my heart speed up, and my palms are so slippery I can hardly hold my quarterly. My lips begin to feel like great, wet zucchinis.

Just before my turn, the lady next to me clasps her hands to her head and exclaims, "I've got a migraine. I pass."

Suddenly I have to take her verse, the long-

and True

or the Hot-Air Forum

est verse in the text, and it's filled with 12-syllable Oriental words. I feel a migraine coming on, but I open my mouth and begin. What comes out is a whispery, twittery sound like that of a three year old saying his Mother's Day piece.

As soon as I'm done reading my verse, I quickly count the remaining verses to see if I'm going to have to read yet another verse this hour. Heaven forbid.

A Better Way

The Round Robin is not a wrong method, but it could be improved. For one thing, I wish teachers would assign everyone a verse at the beginning of the lesson. "Ron, take verse one, and Lisa, verse two," and so on. Then he could give us five minutes to look over our text before the lesson starts. During this time he could take up the offering and take attendance. It would also help if he would put on the chalkboard the pronunciations of big words in the text, and take a few moments to go over them. Whenever a student has a migraine or asthma attack, he himself should take that student's verse, so that the order of verses is not interrupted.

Finally, a good teacher would encourage students to add the "personal" to their Scripture texts by inserting some of their own remarks, or by quizzing them with questions such as, "How do you feel about that verse?" or "Have you ever had an experience that illustrates that verse?"

The Talking Head

The teacher who uses this method takes a deep breath at the beginning of the hour and then begins a one-hour monologue delivered with the sparkle of a coconut. Often he reads word for word from the quarterly, including page numbers and instructions to the teacher. He never looks up to see if anyone has a question or comment, because he really doesn't want to be interrupted.

For a few minutes we students pretend that this method is all right, perhaps even ideal. After all, it takes the heat off of us, and if the lesson author was good, the teacher might even be tolerable.

But after twenty minutes of this mumble-logue, a strange mood comes over the class. Heads begin to tilt and bodies sag into the pews. Spiders begin weaving webs between students. Old men switch their hearing aids from "amplify" to "The Cosby Show." One old lady takes off her glasses and begins to clean them over and over again until you think she has rubbed a hole through the lens. A middle-aged man opens his billfold and begins to clean and sort its contents on the pew beside him. One student reaches for a church bulletin, which he rolls into tiny pieces and stuffs into his ears. An attractive lady borrows a pocket knife and begins to do her manicure, and a crude man next to her is practicing covert nasal explorations.

A Better Way

Ideally we could replace all "talking heads" with someone who has the looks of Kevin Costner, the brains of Carl Sagan, the voice of Tom Brokaw, the fascination of Paul Harvey, and the humor of Jay Leno. Unfortunately it's not as easy as you might think to find these types of teachers.

To divide is to conquer the problem of monologue. Anything that will break up the singsong pattern of his lecture will save the hour from a living death.

If you are a talking-head teacher, think of

your lecture as three small lectures instead of one long one. At each break, insert something radically different from your familiar voice. For example, you might pause and play from a tape cassette a bit of a popular song that illustrates your point. Or show the class a picture of something you've been talking about such as a picture of Solomon's temple or a magazine picture of someone who is practicing the virtue you espouse. You might consider giving students sealed envelopes at the beginning of class. Inside each envelope is a question, a text, or words to a hymn. At the appropriate time, pause in your lecture to let another student open his or her envelope and read his or her "piece."

The Hot-Air Forum

The teacher of this class begins by saying, "Well, what do you wanna talk about today? Anybody got anything he wants to share?"

This type of invitation opens the door to everything from politics to sex. Usually the same three people talk every Sunday—the ones with the strongest opinions and the strongest lungs. The introverts say nothing and may soon transfer to a lecture class, where they can hear something besides blarney and blather.

The Hot-Air Forum can, on occasion, generate a great deal of interest and attention. Unfortunately that can be dangerous. Some of the questions and comments that arise are simply surreptitious "messages" to someone sitting across the way. For example, "What do you do with someone who always tries to run the church board?" Or, "Why doesn't anyone around here ask the women's opinion of how to do things?"

Some remarks may be so confessional they would make Dr. Ruth blush. "What do you do when your wife is in menopause and she's driving you crazy?" Or, "What do you do with a husband who leaves his dirty underwear lying around the house?"

The trouble with these carbon-dioxide conventions is that many topics are raised and discussed, but seldom are solutions found. Often the Bible is not even consulted in reference to the problems. Students leave class feeling relieved of some inner tensions but just as confused as ever about how to solve their situations.

A Better Way

If you are a teacher who likes discussion, try adding a little bit of structure and order to the sessions. For example, use a printed handout with questions on it, so that the class can stay on track. Instead of hoping for good topics, have the class select topics in advance for the entire quarter, perhaps by using a questionnaire. Consider dividing the class hour in half. The first half is spent talking about problems; the second half is for discussing biblical solutions.

If you are a fan of the tried and true methods, it's not necessary to abandon your methods in order to improve your teaching. A little fine-tuning can make even ordinary methods into extraordinary tools of teaching.

Chapter 7

The Visual Advantage

Words, words, words, I'm so sick of words . . .
if you're in love, show me.
—My Fair Lady

Visuals Connect

I hardly need to convince you of the importance of visuals in communications in this video age. Audiovisuals are as necessary to today's classroom as desks and chairs. Even so, it's helpful to look at some of the specific ways that visuals help in communication.

Visuals help the teacher learn the material himself. To understand fully any given lesson material, you need to be able to see it in your imagination. The process of translating verbal information into visual information gives the teacher a special grasp of truth. When you can *see* it, you are ready to teach it.

You can also share this process with your students. For example, you can give each of your students a piece of paper or a transparency and markers and ask them to visualize the day's lesson text using stick figures, lines, shapes, or whatever. Then project or post their visualizations and see just how much all of you learn from the process. Students will *visualize* the same passage in many different ways, and the variety will be stimulating.

Visuals clarify concepts. Imagine two sculptors talking to each other on the telephone. One of them is in New York City and the other is in Alabama. The one in New York is a teacher of sculpture, and the one in Alabama is his student. As the teacher works on a sculpture, he tells his student each step of the procedure.

"OK, now take a little chip off the cheek, next to the nose."

Just how good would the pupil's sculpture look? How much would it resemble his teacher's ideal, if the teacher used only words to teach?

In a similar way, Christian teachers are fooling themselves if they think that they can teach complex metaphysical concepts such as reconciliation and humility, using nothing but words. Young minds need to see a picture of a husband and wife hugging to understand reconciliation, or a picture of someone carrying suitcases to illustrate humility.

Teaching about the God-man who lived two thousand years ago in a foreign country requires the use of visuals to overcome the barriers of time and space. Bible vocabulary such as "repentance" and "baptism" need more than verbalization to be meaningful to an age whose language is under constant revision and full of slang.

Visuals open other channels. Recent research has shown that people learn through different channels and in different styles. Some people learn primarily through listening to words. They would rather play a taped book than read a book. Others learn by hands-on experience and prefer to *do,* rather than listen or watch. Some learn primarily through the visual channel. They like to watch videos and slides to learn. Still others learn by interacting with other people in discussion. By using audiovisuals, a teacher increases his chances of communicating with everyone and of holding everyone's interest.

Visuals save time. Of course it takes time to make visuals, but using visual aids saves *class* time. And since most Sunday schools have very limited time in which to teach, a good teacher will want to be as efficient as possible. One picture is worth a thousand words, and the right picture is worth considerably more. A portion of a video can make clear what might take days to explain and illustrate. A chart can summarize weeks of research. A simple transparency on the overhead or a handout of the same material can give students access to material that would take students many hours to figure out on their own.

Why the Scarcity?

If visuals are so valuable, why don't more teachers use them? There are many reasons or *excuses* why teachers neglect visual aids. Here are a few of them.

Teachers have had bad experiences. They remember the time a projector bulb went out and embarrassed them, or the time the flannel board was caught by the wind and blew over. So they decide, "Never again!"

Some teachers have unrealistic expectations. They try to produce professional quality posters, videos, or audiotapes, and it takes so much time and money that they give up and never try again.

Some teachers lack confidence. Not being artsy-craftsy they shy away from anything that would require art skills. They feel it's too much trouble to delegate this, so they simply don't use visuals.

Many lack training. Some teachers have had no training in visual usage and no good models to imitate. This is a problem that can be remedied if a church will sponsor a hands-on training session now and then.

There are teachers who have ego problems. Some teachers seem to want all the attention focused on themselves and appear to resent giving up talk time to use a visual or audio aid. Others are afraid of appearing "wimpy," feeling that only women and children are into artsy-craftsy things.

All these problems can be tamed by proper training in the availability and usage of visuals.

Doing It Right

Sloppy visual presentations are probably worse than using no visuals at all. That does not mean that visuals must be expensive or professional to be well received.

Here are some basic principles to keep in mind when planning a visual presentation.

Less is more. The more equipment and the more software, the more likely that things will go wrong. If one slide projector will do the job, use just one instead of five. Even the simplest visual aids cost time and money, so use only enough to do the job. This will free you for other equally important parts of teaching—Bible study, prayer time, fellowship with students, and lesson planning.

Visuals should aid instruction and not supplant it. The purpose of visuals is not to show off teacher skills or even to dazzle students with technology and talent. This is not said to disparage excellence but to emphasize instruction over showmanship. Your purpose is to teach, not to impress.

Visuals should clarify not confuse. When making transparencies, posters, etc., that contain lettering, stay away from fancy styles that are difficult to read. Use short telegraph sentences rather than eloquent paragraphs. Six lines of no more than six words per line is a good rule for transparencies. Aim to be readable, not clever.

If using a slide show, use background music that your students recognize rather than an unfamiliar song that only puzzles them.

Practice for smoothness. A smooth presentation usually just takes a little rehearsing, not great talent. If a presentation is sloppy, student attention will stray from the message to your entertaining mistakes. If necessary, get an assistant to help you make it go smoothly, or practice at home until you've got it right.

Participation visuals are usually superior to impression visuals. It's one thing to hold up a poster for your students to read. It's quite another thing to have them help you by making the posters themselves. Students tend to remember what they *do* more than what they see. A video shown by the teacher will have less impact than a video made by the students. Even so, both impression and participation visuals are good. Use both.

Inexpensive visuals are often preferable to expensive ones. Remember, your purpose in the classroom is not to compete with the theater or the sports and entertainment industry. Your purpose is to instruct, and you can do that without breaking your budget and your back.

Here are some of the expensive visual aids compared with economical ones. If you can get by with the inexpensive, do so.

Expensive Visuals	Economical Visuals
videos and video projectors	role plays/informal drama
slides and filmstrips	visual boards
field trips	interest centers
computers and projection panels	crafts/artwork
multimedia productions	overhead transparencies
printed literature/handouts	simple puppets
cassettes/CDs	sandboxes/dioramas
professional puppets	games/activities/contests
commercial magic/chemistry	magazine-tearing activities
full-costume drama	posters/charts/flash cards

However, some of the expensive visuals are not so costly if you can raise the money or share the equipment. Some of it lasts a long time and is relatively inexpensive on an hours-used basis.

Why the emphasis on inexpensive visuals? Aside from obvious stewardship reasons, there are practical reasons. It has been shown that teachers tend to use visuals only if they are available and relatively inexpensive and simple to use. To encourage visual use, keep the productions free or inexpensive.

Furthermore, many of the most powerful visuals tend to be the participation visuals that are on the economical list. If a role play will do the job, why invest in a costly video that portrays professional actors? Students will remember their own role play longer than one by Tom Cruise or Robert Redford.

Recommended Visuals

It would be impossible to survey all the types of visual aids in one chapter, especially with new ones coming into existence all the time. Some of the newer visual aids and some of the more universal old standbys are presented here.

Video

Most churches have developed a library of videos, and some churches have an exchange feature with other church libraries in the area. Institutions such as Good News Productions (2111 N. Main; Box 22; Joplin, MO 64802) also offer videos on a variety of topics, and local commercial video stores often carry some religious videos.

When using a video in the classroom, be sure you have previewed it carefully. These days you might find almost anything in a video—yes, even religious videos. It could be rather embarrassing if you have not previewed the tape.

How can you use video in the classroom?

1. It's probably not wise to use a video for an entire classroom hour. Play a portion of it to supplement your teaching, and the rest of it at the next session.

Keep in mind that young people have been brought up on videos, so they are rather choosy in what they will watch. A "talking head" video (see *Fine-Tuning the Tried and True*) or one that's poorly done will likely do more harm than good at creating a good impression.

2.   For discussion starters, you might play a portion of a program taped off the air, perhaps a talk show; or you might tape an interview with a visiting missionary or special personality and play part of that for your class.

3.   Include a video as part of an interest center for students to play. Give them a handout of questions to be answered by watching the tape.

4.   Show your class selections of a Christian convention you attended or a survey of a mission field that they are supporting.

5.   Some subjects such as sexuality or alcohol recovery are so personal that they are not suitable for classroom discussion. Videos are available that your students can take home and view or view with a support group.

6.   Student-made videos represent one of the best ways to instruct and apply the Scriptures. Give students a camcorder, and ask them to make a one-minute commercial promoting clean living or church attendance; or ask them to role-play a Bible story, while one of them captures it on camera for later review and discussion. Then stand back as they amaze you with their abilities!

7.   If you know you are going to be absent some Sunday, tape yourself teaching the lesson—complete with visuals and cuts of question and answer or interview. Leave the video for a substitute teacher.

8.   Dress up as a Bible character and let students tape an interview of you for playback and discussion.

Video Projection

Video projectors are very expensive and beyond the budget of individual teachers. But a church can purchase one, and teachers can share it.

Advantages? The large picture produced by a video projector tends to create more emotional impact on the class. Students will tend to whisper less during the showing, and the large screen shows details that would be missed in a television showing. Some video projectors will also project computer graphics which opens up other possibilities for an innovative teacher.

Computers

Although expensive, a computer or two in a church classroom can help fill a gap in instruction by providing some individualized instruction for early arrivals or for special sessions. How can a computer be used to assist your instruction?

1. Drill and mastery learning. When teaching the books of the Bible, let students drill themselves at the computer.

2. True-to-life situations. Let students apply the lesson by reading a computerized "situation" and selecting correct responses. The responses can be programmed to correct errors or to give additional information.

3. Learning centers. A computer is a kind of learning center by itself. If teaching about the creation, set up a table with items from creation and use a computer program to drill students in the days of creation.

4. Teacher training. Prepare a program for training teachers, and show it at a teacher conference. Make it available for take-home too.

5. Record keeping. A computer can also be used for keeping attendance and offering records and for analyzing student progress.

Computer Projection Panels

Electronic projection panels are available to lay on the stage of your overhead projector or attach to your slide projector so that you can project whatever is in your computer. As of this writing, they are rather expensive and vary a great deal in quality of performance. A church or several teachers could go together to purchase one and share it. You can prepare all your visuals at home on your PC, and there isn't the cost and bother of making overhead transparencies. After class, students can borrow the disk to review the lesson on the learning center computer.

Caution: With all the new electronic genies, there comes the temptation to let the machines do the teaching. Resist this temptation, because all electronic mediums create a certain amount of "psychological distance." Students need more than machines to grow. They need to interact with each other and the teacher. They need to learn to handle their Bibles and to participate in learning projects. Electronics no longer have the charisma they did when they first came out. Many of today's students are well trained in media usage but lack in personal attention and social skills. Only a real live teacher can give students the affection and attention they crave and need for growth.

Old Standbys

Some visual aids seem to wear quite well in spite of the new-comers to the field. Lets look at some of them.

Visual Boards

1. Chalkboards are available in almost any color you wish, from a good commercial supplier. Recently the whiteboard seems to have replaced the traditional green or black chalkboard because of the availability of dry erase markers. You can make your own whiteboard with a piece of bathroom paneling from the lumberyard. (Marlite is one brand.) You can fasten it to your classroom wall with screws or frame it in wood and use it on an easel.

After much use, the board will develop a haze, which can be removed with a special commercial liquid or with lacquer thinner, followed by powdered household cleanser on a sponge.

Dry erase markers are available at office supply stores. Be careful to keep the lids on markers, for they tend to dry out quickly when exposed to air.

2. Bulletin boards represent one of the very best ways to teach. Bulletin board displays can be set up in advance of class and can *teach* while you go about your classroom work. One of the best uses of bulletin boards is to have your students prepare a bulletin board display that illustrates the lesson or unit.

3. Flannel boards are still used by teachers of the very young. Newer commercial materials tend to be more colorful, and come in a larger format.

The simple genius of visual boards is that they are always there. Visuals that are easily available are the ones that teachers most often use. Don't overlook these boards in your fascination with newer technology. Electronic chalkboards now print out the information in handout form and even transmit it over telephone lines. These are beyond the budget of Sunday school teachers, but any teacher can afford a chalkboard or even make one for himself.

Overhead Projectors

These projectors have been around for a long time now and still offer one of the best approaches for daily instructional use. Materials have been greatly improved to make it possible for the average teacher to produce professional, quality materials for projection. Most plain paper copiers will make transparencies at a modest cost, sometimes in colors. You can also make quality transparencies on your personal computer printer.

One simple way to use an overhead is to buy fine-point dry erase markers that are made for whiteboards. You can write directly on the stage of the projector with these, and they will erase with a light touch of a rag or tissue. This saves you the cost of transparencies. Some other kinds of markers can be erased with just a damp rag such as china markers and vis-a-vis markers. Even crayons will wipe off with a damp rag, but they print only a black line no matter which color you use. Eyebrow pencils are excellent for overhead projection, and they too will erase from the stage or acetate with a damp cloth.

One of the best ways to use an overhead is to give students small pieces of acetate (cut a transparency into fourths) and a marker or crayon. Then ask them to draw or write something on it. For example, if teaching about stewardship, ask the students to write down how much money they think a Christian can make before becoming "rich." Collect and project these as a readiness activity for the lesson.

Paper Graphics

Paper still represents one of the most inexpensive and effective types of visuals available. Here are some types.

1. Students can make posters to illustrate the lesson, or you can make them in advance.

2. Several students can work at a wall covered with art paper. Let them put a Bible story on the mural, or use it as a graffiti board to record their thoughts about the lesson.

3. Tear off strips of adding machine tape and give to students for recording Bible verses. Then display their tapes on the wall.

4. Prepare your lesson points on a flip chart. You can make one of these with a large tablet or by tying together several sheets of poster paper.

5. Homemade flash cards can serve to present your lesson outline, review lessons, or provide vocabulary study for your class. Using them with the entire class keeps all lookers on their toes. "What if he calls on me?!"

6. Maps can be projected onto a large sheet of paper using an overhead projector. Students can then write in names and places and trace journeys.

7. It's hard to beat simple flat pictures for teaching children about the dress and culture of life in Bible times. Publishers are

upgrading their pictures according to recent knowledge of Bible-time culture, and many pictures in books can be passed around or shown with an overhead projector. A new type of opaque projector uses a small video camera with attached lights to project opaque copy onto a television screen. It is rather expensive but would be quite useful with a large class.

Puppets

Children never seem to tire of making and using puppets, which are one of the best participation visuals. Your local library will have dozens of books describing all kinds of homemade puppets, from simple paper dolls to elaborate fabric puppets.

Audio Tapes and CDs

In the rush to use video tapes, many teachers have overlooked the lingering value of audio cassettes. They are especially effective with young children whose imaginations could rival anything ever shown on the big screen. Children need practice in listening, and a cassette gives them practice.

Adults also can benefit from an audio tape, especially if you first give them a handout or project a transparency that coordinates with the audio. Here are some other ways a cassette recorder can be used.

1. Let a prerecorded tape read the Scripture to the class. You might even put some sound effects on the tape for fun and interest.

2. Put a quiz on audio tape to be used at a learning center.

3. Give students a blank tape and a recorder and a children's Bible story book. Have them read the story to the tape, adding sound effects as they go.

4. Play bits of popular songs from your cassette or CD that illustrate points in your lesson. It is also helpful to print the words on a handout.

5. Let students read the Bible into a cassette. Then play it back for memory work practice.

6. Tape your teaching, if you dare. Listen to yourself for evaluation.

Getting Visual

One of the biggest challenges teachers face is knowing what to visualize. Here are some tips.

Suppose you are teaching the Christmas story. What should you visualize? Here are three suggestions.

Visualize the nouns—persons, places, and things—in the text. In this case you might visualize the manger, the special star, a map of the journey of the wise men, frankincense and myrrh, swaddling clothes, etc.

Visualize the plot. Outline the plot of the story on paper, then decide how best to show it—perhaps a chalkboard outline, or a series of pictures, or a puppet show of the story.

Visualize the truths. The Christmas story contains many truths worthy of underlining with visuals. Choose the truths that best support your lesson aim, and use visuals to impress them on your students. For example, the truth, "God in the flesh," might make a good overhead transparency. Outline a man. Then show God "pouring himself" into the man, and label it "Jesus, the God-man." You might choose the truth, "Mary's humility made her useful," in which case you might illustrate with a gadget or machine that works and one that doesn't. A typewriter that yields to the touch is a machine that is useful, for example.

Visual Eggs

Confessions About a Few Scrambled

S eldom have I seen a teacher use visual aids without having problems. As an instructor of audiovisuals, I have laid my own share of visual eggs.

One time, for example, I was demonstrating how to set up a projection screen. "Screens are tricky," I warned the class, as I tried to spread open the legs of the tripod with my foot. I kicked and pried at the legs vigorously. Suddenly they snapped open, catching my foot inside the aluminum trap. I lost my balance, and on my way to the floor I smacked my chin on the screen with a solid "whock." The screen landed on top of me. I jumped up quickly, trying to act as if this were normal. There were muffled sounds of appreciation from the class as I righted myself and went on talking.

"Now the hard part," I added, "is getting the main shaft to lift up to its full height. It tends to stick as a rule." This time it didn't stick. The shaft shot up like a frightened frog, striking two long fluorescent bulbs on the ceiling, raining down glass confetti and poisonous gas on all of us. At the same time, the screen retracted into the case with a "zwish" and a "crack," the crack being the sound fingers make when they break. This time the sounds of appreciation were no longer muffled. I laughed too, unable to admit I needed hospitalization and counseling.

essons

Teaching teachers to use visuals isn't as simple as it might seem. An adult teacher came to me once, asking advice on how to get started with visuals. "I'm not very good with my hands," Jack said, and I could see why. He was an odd man who appeared to have been made of parts from several different people, with hands added as an afterthought.

"Why don't you try the flannel board?" I suggested. "Just put your main points on strips of poster board and stick them to the board as you speak." I felt safe recommending the flannel board, since it has no moving parts or bulbs to blow out.

Sunday morning. Jack set up his board and began the lesson. When he came to his first main point, he confidently placed the first strip on the board. My heart sank. He had written his words with a number-two pencil, nearly invisible more than a foot away. He smoothed out the strip and turned back to his notes. The strip fluttered noiselessly to the floor. Quickly I realized he didn't know the strips wouldn't stick without some kind of flocking on the back. Each time he calmly placed a strip on the board, it aviated straight to the floor.

Had I been Jack, I would have died of embarrassment, but not Jack. He went right on building a mountain of cardboard on the floor, proud that he was finally teaching with visual aids.

Projected visuals are a regular nest for visual eggs. A former student of mine called me from the mission field for some advice. "I'm making up a slide show to send the churches," he said, "but I can't remember how you said to let the operator know when to advance each slide."

"Well," I replied, "one good way to is to take a drinking glass and lightly tap it with a spoon to create a tiny 'ping.'" He thanked me for that intellectual diamond and went to work.

A few weeks later, I was visiting a church where his slides were being shown with taped narration. Sure enough, he had used a drinking glass and a spoon, only he must have placed the microphone inside the glass. The spoon he swung with an arm that would have made Babe Ruth look like a wimp, and the sound that came out resembled someone striking a china bathtub with a tire iron. Babies began to cry, and grown-ups in the audience looked at each other with eyes I've seen only in the movie *Holocaust.* One hundred twenty pings later, we struggled out of church to seek treatment.

I am sometimes consoled when I see one of my superiors slip up. One of my university professors began showing a filmstrip in class. At first the frames and words didn't seem to match. "Perhaps I am behind a frame," she mumbled, and she flipped forward to catch up. As time went on, the pictures seemed to make more sense, as we strained to find some symbolic meaning where there was none. But as the filmstrip continued, it became crystal clear that she had put on the wrong tape for this filmstrip. We began murmuring among ourselves, hoping she would get the hint and stop this sham, but she steadily flipped through all eighty-five frames. When it was over, she said meekly, "This filmstrip wasn't nearly as good as I remembered it." We assured her it was indeed an unforgettable filmstrip.

Whenever I give my students in methods class a chance to practice storytelling, it seems to bring out the best in them. One dedicated girl created an elaborate diorama to help her tell the story of Old Testament sacrifices. The two-by-three-foot box was colorfully painted in detail. In it she placed tiny dolls to represent worshipers and a small altar made of real stones with pine sticks on top of the altar. As she explained the sacrifices, she laid a toy animal on the altar, squirted it with charcoal lighter, and lit it. It was truly beautiful, and the class "oohed" and "aahed" her creativity.

Then the fire grew brighter. Soon the entire diorama glowed a bright orange. Then it turned black, and finally it collapsed into a pile of gray-orange ashes. The room filled with smoke, and students rushed to beat out the embers with their notebooks. It was more sacrifice than she intended, but worth every minute of it—if only for the excitement it created in class.

One day a boy came to me for advice about the story he was planning to tell in class. "I would like to do the one about the storm on the Sea of Galilee where Jesus calmed the waves," he explained. "I'm going to use a pan of water with a boat in it, but do you know any way to make the water bubble?"

"Oh," I answered offhandedly, "you might drop in a piece of dry ice, or add a little vinegar and baking soda."

His eyes lit up. "Thanks!" He disappeared down the hallway.

When it was his turn to present his story, he slipped out of the room momentarily and then returned, staggering under a pan of water that could float two aircraft carriers. In it he set a large paper boat loaded with paper dolls of Jesus and his disciples. As I stared unbelieving, he dumped in an entire bottle of white vinegar, filling the room with a pickle smell. Next he stationed a friend at the light switch, with instructions for him to turn it on and off rapidly, simulating lightning. Another friend was planted just out of sight behind the classroom door. He was holding a large sheet of tin that he was supposed to rattle with all his might, imitating thunder.

When the student came to the storm part of his tale, he dumped a double handful of

But the worst visual egg I've ever seen was laid by a perfectly capable Sunday school teacher. Although she studied her lesson and made an effort to be interesting, she never used a visual aid for fear of making a fool of herself. Not even the chalkboard that hung inches away from her. That is the worst visual egg any teacher could ever lay. Better to have a little egg on your face than to scramble a lesson.

soda into the water. Instantly the water began to boil and gurgle. One nameless student began humming "Master, the Tempest Is Raging." The paper ship listed and then headed straight for the bottom of the pan, drowning everyone, including the Master of wind and waves. At the same time, thunder began rumbling outside, sounding suspiciously like someone jumping up and down on the hood of a car. Then the lights began to flash off and on, strobe-like.

Meanwhile, the vinegar was far from spent, and the foam boiled up over the sides of the pan and down the sides of the desk as we watched helplessly. By now everyone in class was screaming with pleasure, clutching their stomachs, and wiping big tears from their eyes. Then suddenly everything went black. The light keeper had blown a circuit breaker. When at last the laughter died down, we could still hear "thundermaker" out in the hallway doing his thing, unaware that the Lord of the sea had long ago joined the crabs and clams at the bottom of the ocean.

The fact that this student dropped out of school a week later is only a coincidence, I am sure.

Chapter 8

Room Service

There are two teachers in your class—
YOU and YOUR ROOM.

WHILE YOU ARE TEACHING, the walls of your room are also teaching. The beauty of your room says something about God and you. Ugliness says something else about neglect and carelessness. The mood for learning and how students feel about Sunday school are both largely determined by the environment of your room.

Some teachers have little choice about their classrooms. They are assigned to makeshift rooms and are forbidden to even tack a picture to the wall. Some are relegated to dingy corners of the basement, there to compete with toads and water bugs and mildew. You may be one of these unfortunate teachers.

On the other hand, there's a good chance you can do something to improve your room in spite of its weaknesses. Perhaps you can make it less dreary, less crowded, less forbidding. If so, it will be worth the efforts.

What are the most important features of a good classroom?

Space

Is your classroom three-quarters full?
Then it's full.
Church growth studies have shown that when a class is nearly full, then attendance levels off or even declines. No matter how

many prospects you visit, your class will probably not grow beyond its space limits. Furthermore, if you are going to use any method besides lecture, you will likely need more space in which to rearrange chairs and tables.

The ideal classroom should contain approximately the following square feet per student.

Preschool Age Children	30-35 square feet
Elementary Age Children	25-30 square feet
Teens	20-25 square feet
Adults	10-15 square feet

Sound impossible? Perhaps. But no matter what size your room, you can increase your space with some minor adjustments.

Try installing only wall-mounted furniture. Use wall cabinets instead of floor cabinets or a chalkboard fastened to the wall instead of on an easel.

Teaching small children? Consider removing all furniture from the room. Let students sit on blocks of foam rubber or boat seat cushions or carpet samples. Provide them with homemade lap desks made of slabs of plywood or Masonite.

Teaching older students? Use folding chairs and tables that can be moved out of the way for activities. Use a roll-away cart for supplies, storing it in the hallway except when needed. Use a room divider when you need to divide your class into two small groups. A curtain will do, or you can make a wallboard divider that will hug the wall when not in use.

Sometimes a simple rearrangement of the chairs will create more space. I've found that I can get more school desks into my college classroom by putting them in a large circle around the walls. If you have a square room, consider arranging your chairs in diamond fashion. This eliminates large back rows, where students like to hide out from the teacher and create a commotion.

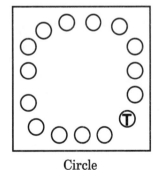

Circle

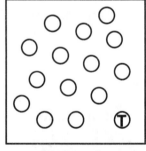

Diamond

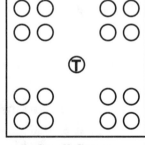

Small Group
Activities

If you still lack space, perhaps it's time to find another teacher and another classroom, and divide your class in half. Try locating a church member who lives right near the church, and ask to use his living room or basement den as a classroom. Summertime? Take the kids outdoors in good weather. If teaching cooperative adults, try reserving the conference room at a nearby local fast-food restaurant.

Beauty

Your classroom doesn't have to be the Taj Mahal, but it does need to be cheerful and inviting. "Beauty is practical," Robert Schuller noted, "because beauty is inspirational."

Light is the most cheerful thing you can put into your class-room. Do you need brighter light bulbs? A new window shade that works? Perhaps you just need to paint the room a lighter color.

Consider asking an artist church member to paint one wall of your classroom in a beautiful seascape or other nature scene. Or visit a department store or photo store, and see what's available in the way of commercial murals that apply to the wall like wall-paper. Hanging a large mirror or mirror tiles on one wall can create a sense of a larger room.

Walls represent valuable teaching space as well as beauty. One teacher I know made child-level chalkboards all the way around her classroom so students could practice writing memory work. She made the boards by painting hardboard Masonite with flat latex house paint, available in many colors.

Hang a large piece of art paper on one wall, and you have a graffiti wall that students can use to express their ideas about the lesson. Put an inspirational verse or theme on it, and invite early arrivals to record their feelings and ideas.

A wall-sized bulletin board covered in bright fabric will provide you with a medium for illustrating your lesson. A prepared display on it will "teach" while you talk. Let students help you make the display as an application of a given lesson. Provide them with materials, ideas, and over-the-shoulder help.

Is your room clean? No matter who messed up your room, and no matter how poorly the janitor does his job, the point is, your room needs to be clean. Clean it! It's funny that some teachers who are so picky about the condition of their own home will tolerate mess and stench when it comes to their classrooms.

Comfort

Your classroom represents a "home away from home" for your students. Young children in particular can find Sunday school stressful, and a comfortable room can help ease separation anxiety. What can you do to create comfort?

Young children should be located fairly close to the auditorium when possible, to give them easy access to their parents in emergencies.

Child-sized furniture makes "sitting for an hour" a lot easier. Here are recommended chair seat heights:

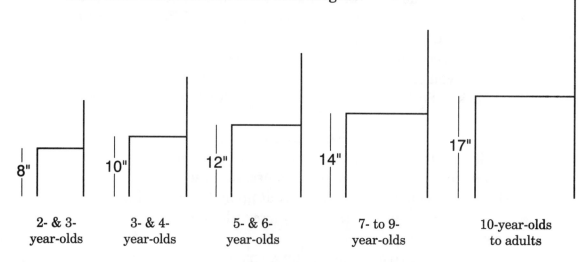

2- & 3- year-olds	3- & 4- year-olds	5- & 6- year-olds	7- to 9- year-olds	10-year-olds to adults
8"	10"	12"	14"	17"

(Table tops should be approximately ten inches higher than seat bottoms.)

Young children are comforted by the familiar. Resist the urge to change your classroom decor every week. Students get used to having certain things in certain places. Help students feel like they belong by labeling coat racks or mailboxes with their names. One teacher asks each parent to bring some familiar toy or object from home to leave in the room at all times—as a kind of security blanket for the child.

Teaching teens? What do teenagers' rooms look like at home? No, I'm not suggesting you cover the walls of your classroom with rock star pictures, or install truck-sized speakers for your tape player. But some kind of poster would be nice, and something familiar would make them glad to be there.

In short, just follow the golden rule and design your classroom to meet the nature and needs of your students—even adults. It will pay off in increased attendance and improved attitudes.

Health and Safety

Teachers are responsible for the children in their classrooms. If something happens "on your watch," you will have to answer for it. Here are some simple things to consider when prepping your room for teaching children.

1. Do you have enough workers to keep an eye on everyone? The younger the age group, the more workers needed. As many as one worker per three children are necessary in some cases.

2. Is the paint on your walls, furniture, and toys safe to eat? Children love to put things in their mouths. Are things clean? Safe?

3. Are electrical outlets covered? Extension cords taped down? Any heavy lamps or electrical equipment that could be pulled over?

4. Are furniture knobs glued tight? Any splinters or rough corners? Unstable three-legged stools? Rocking chairs that pinch fingers and toes?

5. Are there any loose rugs that could slip? Wastebaskets covered to keep curious children out? Toy box with hinged lids that can pinch fingers?

6. Do you have a first aid kit? Sawdust for vomit? Paper towels for nosebleeds?

7. How about your own attire? Do you wear earrings that could be pulled off and eaten? A brooch that could stick a child's eye when you hug him? A purse with prescription medicines in it?

8. While children are in your classroom, they are your responsibility. It is also your responsibility to see that children are returned safely to their parents. Be careful about releasing your students to friends, brothers and sisters, or anyone you don't know and trust. In these days of child neglect and abuse, you can't be too careful. If a child slips through the cracks, wanders off, or gets hurt, you may be held responsible.

Apples of Gold . . .

Set in Sawdust

When I was growing up, Sunday school often inspired me to jump off a bridge. Only the sweet sound of the closing bell saved me from an early grave. It wasn't the lesson or the teacher that depressed me. It was the classroom.

"The Crater," we called it, since it was only a damp cavity in the dark basement. It featured one tiny window that someone had thoughtfully covered with cardboard, lest some depraved student see a spark of sunlight and bolt for freedom. Our only sun was a forty-watt bulb that dangled from the ceiling and glowed like a burnt-out angel. It was all the light our eyes could stand after being in the dark for so long.

The sludge-gray walls hosted a fungus that grew larger and darker each Sunday. In fact, a wild kingdom of creatures was attracted to our classroom by the moisture: centipedes, slugs, waterbugs, and now and then a dazed snake. On rainy days our room gurgled, and a mini Amazon flowed through the center of the room. It soon carried our paper boats to a mass shipwreck in the corner.

Someone had salvaged some chairs for us from a deceased funeral home. "Groan Valley Memorials" it said on the wooden slats of each chair, and they seemed to go well with the army surplus table. If we didn't sit death still on the chairs, the slats would pinch us where it hurt most. One chair was broken, and we reserved it for unsuspecting visitors. Our will to live returned when we watched some naive visitor collapse into a wooden sandwich on the floor. Seldom did visitors return.

For visual aids we relied on a cheerful, sooty blackboard that leaned on a broken tripod. Halfway through each lesson it fell off, and we used to take bets on the precise moment of its collapse. No one had seen any chalk since the Civil War so it was not in any danger of wearing out.

The teacher's lectern was a homemade hat tree with a crew cut, and it rocked back and forth as he shifted from leg to leg like an ice skater. For storage we used an abandoned church pew that had grown to the wet wall. It had been put there for the overflow crowd that never came, so we buried it under cast-off literature and unclaimed clothing.

I knew other classrooms just as wonderful as that one. Budgettown, Kentucky, for example. There the basement was curtained off into four classes. Since the curtains were made of gauze, I could tune in on the adult teacher or the senior high discussion whenever I got bored with my own teacher—or throw paper wads over the wire into the old folks' class.

At Gnawbone, Indiana, we met in the drip-dry room just off from the baptistery. Freshly dunked converts came there to stand in a wash tub and drain dry. You can't imagine the inspiration of spending an hour with hip boots and yellowed baptismal robes.

At Mapdot, Illinois, we met in an unheated house a block away from the church. After opening exercises we were supposed to run happily down the street to that refrigerator for our class. On cold mornings we left the church at the speed of a fire drill in a nursing home.

At Ricketyville, Michigan, we met in the loft of a barn. Our first duty each Sunday was to scrape pigeon pearls and rodent raisins off our chairs. What a treat that was.

But I give the prize to Dumptruck, Iowa, where we met in a converted coal bin. Termites had made high-rise apartments in the support columns, and each week the piles of sawdust grew larger. We kept one eye on the ceiling at all times.

In spite of it all, we had some wonderful teachers in these classrooms. They were great storytellers and Scripture quoters, and they truly cared about us. But in these surroundings they were like apples of gold set in sawdust. We listened to them, and we learned. But along with the lesson for the day we learned that Sunday school was dismal and dirty. We smelled like mildew after class and we strained to think of some good reason to return next week. We began to feel that the Creator was opposed to beauty and comfort,

and we concluded that Sunday school was the bargain barn of the church.

In recent years I have visited hundreds of churches in the heartland of America, and the change I have seen in classrooms is a miracle of color and light. Teachers have caught on that "the walls teach." Bright murals spangle the walls of modern classrooms. Giant bulletin boards silently teach the text while the teacher drones on. The noise that used to be labeled "discipline problem" has been muffled by carpets, curtains, and solid furniture. I have seen classrooms equipped as well as any shop or office ever was. One classroom I saw features a large bookrack on wheels, loaded with beautiful books for the children to read. Attractive learning centers are to Sunday school what shopping centers are to the community: centers of supply and fellowship. Adult classes have introduced sofas and decorator furniture. Don't be surprised to find record players, projectors, cassettes, and video tape players available for checkout. Sunday school is growing up.

I am writing this article while sitting in a lovely Sunday school room. The morning sun splashes an amber glow on the pecan-paneled walls. Colorful pictures and Scripture texts dress the walls like jewelry. Up front is a sturdy whiteboard with last week's lesson on it in blue ink. Full-color literature is neatly placed at each student's space on the table. Cheerful fluorescent lights reflect off a white ceiling, giving a clean, fresh look to the tweed carpet. The warm air is perfumed with a new-wood aroma.

The teacher of this class is one of my former education students. She is one of the best I've ever seen—pure gold. And in this classroom she is an "apple of gold set in silver."

Chapter 9

Taking Your Temperature

Hey, we did good!
OOPS, what happened here?
Here come de judge.

BEING EVALUATED sounds ominous. It is something you might like to try to get out of if you can. Maybe you can arrange to have pneumonia that day, or have an urgent call from your cousin in Tokyo?

And yet, teachers are always being evaluated, whether they know it or not. God is always evaluating us, and our students always have opinions of our work. Some teachers criticize themselves unfairly and get discouraged.

Evaluation is a positive word like improvement or quality, and not a negative word like censorship or humiliation. True, the evaluation process is not always like a day at Disneyland®, but in the end, it may leave you feeling quite pleased with yourself.

Why Evaluate?

For a big boost. We all learn by succeeding as well as by failing. Evaluation shows you both your successes and failures. Many teachers are surprised to discover their strengths are showing. Sometimes they don't even know what their strengths are until someone else points them out. Usually their strengths are far more weighty and numerous than their weaknesses.

To get better and better. It's also good to know where your teaching is weak, because such knowledge is the starting point for improvement. Some teachers never get any better because no one will tell them how. If you know your weaknesses, you can get some training or do some reading that will help you tone them down. Many teachers are surprised to find that their weaknesses are slight and can be improved with small changes in procedure or technique, rather than having to completely overhaul their personalities.

To feel included. Students enjoy an opportunity to evaluate their teachers because it makes them feel needed and important. That feeling will help them be better students.

Most of your students will evaluate you fairly, perhaps even generously. There may be one crackpot who puts down everything including the color of your socks. But his remarks are usually obvious in their unfairness. No one student's opinion should be taken too seriously. You will have to decide if your critics are being fair, and discard anything that is immature, or trivial, or just plain wrong.

It's a two-way street. There's always a big fish that eats a little fish, and there's always someone evaluating the evaluator. Nobody gets by without scrutiny.

You may ask your students to evaluate your teaching, but you are always evaluating them too. And all of us are accountable to God.

So the question is not, "Shall we evaluate?" but "*How* shall we evaluate to do the most good?"

How Should We Evaluate?

There are several different ways of evaluating teachers, students, lessons and classrooms.

Some teachers like to appoint a friend to videotape their teaching with a camcorder. Later they can sit down and view the tape in privacy, looking for personality strengths and weaknesses. If you ask a friend or mate to view with you, he or she may point out some things that even you don't see as strengths. "Oh, you look so handsome. You have great posture."

Other teachers find this method of self-evaluation much too threatening. They find that they can't function normally when a camera is watching them, and they loathe watching themselves on tape, seeing only their weaknesses.

Even so, it's a valuable and valid method of weeding out mannerisms and quirks of personality such as poor eye contact and nose-picking.

Some churches feel that self-evaluation is not quite honest. It's like having a mother serve as a judge of a baby contest in which her baby is a contestant.

These churches prefer to assign a mature and educated person to evaluate teachers, students, and classrooms. This person might be the Minister of Education, an elder, or even a committee of three or four persons.

After observing teachers, the evaluator meets with the teachers for interviews and suggestions, and perhaps presents a written list of suggestions for improvement.

If the church has the space, one classroom can be designed as an observation room. Install a window so that an evaluator can watch whatever class is meeting in that room. Parents and prospective teachers may want to spend some time observing too so that they can learn teaching and parenting skills from a capable teacher.

No matter what approach you take to evaluation, it's helpful to have prepared forms to follow, so you will not overlook anything important. The following pages include a number of forms for evaluating yourself, your lesson, and your students. Try one a quarter, or use several now, and then again in six months to see the change.

Telling Yourself the Truth

Read the following statements and circle those that best describe your feelings about your teaching. In the right column, write a more realistic evaluation of yourself and your work.

My Feelings

1. "I'm a total failure as a teacher."

2. "I am so good I amaze myself."

3. "No one appreciates me and all the work I do for this class."

4. "If I were a good teacher, all my students would be perfectly behaved.

5. "I should be able to answer any question my students have."

6. "My students should know without my telling them just how much _____ (behavior) bothers me."

7. "I must cover all the material in the lesson quarterly each week or I haven't done my job."

8. "I'm doing a pretty good job, considering."

9. "I need to be entertaining, charming, and exciting all the time."

10. "If I can't be the best, then I don't want to teach at all."

My Evaluation

Example: "Some of my lectures need more illustration, but I'm usually well-prepared."

Learning From Success

My Biggest Success

Describe your most successful class or class activity this quarter. Write in detail as much as you can remember.

Ideas for Repeating Success

Now analyze what you have written. Where did you go right? What made that session so good? What could you do to repeat this kind of success? Write your ideas in this box.

More Success

Complete the following statements:

1. "The nicest thing any student said to me this quarter was _____
   _____."

2. "I am proud of the way I have _____
   _____."

3. "One thing I like about my personality is _____
   _____."

4. "I can see God working in my life and teaching when _____
   _____."

5. "One of my students who makes me feel most useful is because of the
   way that he/she _____
   _____."

6. "I can feel growth in myself in the area of _____
   _____."

7. "Teaching has brought me closer to God because _____
   _____."

8. "At least I'm not guilty of _____"

9. "One thing that I can do better than a lot of teachers is _____
   _____."

10. "I am more interested in being faithful than successful because _____
    _____."
    _____."

Improving Your Serve

Circle the three areas in the left column that represent your greatest inadequacies. Then in the right column, make a note as to what you can do to get help. If you don't know, ask your Sunday school superintendent, Minister of Education, or education committee.

My Weak Areas

Where I Could Find Help
(i.e., resource persons, books, classes, conventions)

Discipline _____

Lesson Preparation _____

Methods _____

Student Relationships _____

Staff Relationships _____

Visuals _____

Testing and Evaluation _____

Motivation _____

Attitudes _____

Curriculum and Materials _____

Classroom Decor _____

Personal Bible Study _____

Relationship With God _____

Getting Specific

Which of the following methods did you try this quarter? Circle them. Which methods would you like to try next quarter? Check them.

Artwork
Assignments
Audiotapes
Bible Drills
Brainstorming
Bulletin Board Displays
Case Studies
Chalkboard Work
Chemistry, Science Lessons
Chronology Work
Combining With Another Class
Competitions
Computers
Costumes, Dress Up
Creative Writing
Crafts
Debate
Demonstrations
Discussion
Drama, Role play
Field Trips
Finger Plays
Flip Charts
Games
Graffiti Work
Guided Conversation
Handouts
Interviews
Learning Centers
Lecture
Letter Writing
Magic
Making Commercials
Making Slide Shows
Making Videos
Map Work
Meeting Places: Outdoors, Homes, etc.

Memory Work
Models, Dioramas
Music
Musical Instruments
Mysteries, Puzzles
Nature Lessons
Object Lessons
Overhead Transparencies
Panels
Pantomimes, Charades
Photographs and Cameras
Pictures
Posters
Praise and Rewards
Prayer Walk
Printed Literature
Prioritizing Activities
Projects
Puppets
Question and Answer
Questionnaires
Reading Aloud
Reading Great Literature
Real Life Situations
Sandbox
Scrapbooks
Storytelling
Student Reports
Study Teams
Tests
TV Quiz Shows
Video Tapes
Visiting Speakers
Wall Murals
Workbooks
Worship

1. **Did you use enough variety?**

2. **Did you select suitable methods?**

3. **Which methods worked best?**

Check Chart

Check the statements that apply to you.

❑ 1.   I read one book or at least two articles on teaching this year.

❑ 2.   I attended a teacher workshop this year.

❑ 3.   I was on time to class every Sunday.

❑ 4.   I tried at least one new idea in the past quarter.

❑ 5.   I felt prepared most Sundays.

❑ 6.   I spent at least two hours a week preparing my lesson.

❑ 7.   I often go overtime or am done early.

❑ 8.   I solved discipline problems as they came up.

❑ 9.   My attitude was usually good in the classroom.

❑ 10. I dress appropriately for teaching: modest, clean, fitting.

❑ 11. I made contact with each student outside of class—by letter, phone, or a personal visit during the last quarter.

❑ 12. My health condition did not interfere with my teaching.

❑ 13. My class seems responsive and interested.

❑ 14. I gave my students at least one evaluation or test this quarter.

❑ 15. I received more positive feedback than negative from my students and their parents.

❑ 16. I see at least one difference I helped bring about in my students.

❑ 17. I had at least one good laugh per class session.

❑ 18. I went away from most classes feeling good about it.

❑ 19. I see the potential of my students and appreciate it.

❑ 20. I look forward to teaching next quarter/year.

Now analyze each of the above answers and make some notes for improvement. Be as specific as possible, because nothing happens until we get specific.

For the Brave

Do you care what your students think about your teaching? Are you afraid of their opinions? Do you welcome the truth? Make copies of the questionnaire (*My Teacher*) on page 147 and distribute it to your students, if you dare. Let them evaluate you. Whether their opinions are right or wrong, they will appreciate your interest in their thoughts. Be prepared to hear some things you might not want to hear but need to know.

Evaluating Your Success

The best indicator of a teacher's success is the success of his students. From time to time a teacher needs to evaluate his students. Although this is difficult to do and is often subjective, still the process is valuable. With your roll book in hand, evaluate each of your students using the list of questions (*My Students*) on page 148. You may need to get better acquainted with your students in order to answer some of these questions.

Keeping a Record

One way to assure better student evaluations in the future is to keep a notebook on your students. Write interesting things they say and do in the notebook. Put in newspaper clippings of their achievements in school and the community. Include a picture of each student.

Also, make a map of your community. Place a dot on it for each student's home, so that when you need to visit a student, you can do so quickly. Make copies of the map and give it to all your students, so they can know where all their fellow students live. This will help create a sense of community among them.

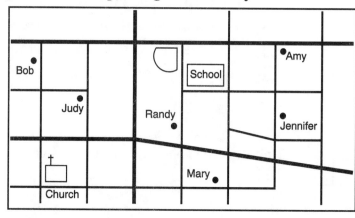

My Teacher

1. What was your favorite class activity or lesson this year and why?

2. Do you feel comfortable in this class? If not, why not?

3. Does the teacher do anything that really irritates you?

4. What is the teacher doing right?

5. What would you like to do more of in this class next quarter?

My Students

1. Which of my students have the worst attendance record? Do I know why?

2. Do all of my students (if mature enough) know how to be saved?

3. Do any of my students need to make a decision for Christ?

4. Have any of my students brought visitors with them?

5. Which of my students are the best behaved? Why?

6. Which of my students are the worst behaved? Why?

7. Are all my students (if mature enough) able to use their Bibles?

8. Which of my students have made an impact for Christ at work or school?

9. Which of my students need extra support because of poor family situations? What am I doing about this?

10. Which of my students are doing poor academically (i.e., reading, writing, etc.)? Do I need to find out why? Can I help?

What if I Flunk Evaluation?

It's possible, but not likely, that you will make a terrible showing in the evaluation of your teaching. What then?

1. Perhaps you need to consider teaching a different age group. You may simply be mismatched with a group that brings out the worst in you.

2. Attend a teacher training or refresher seminar in your area. Try to get specific help for specific weaknesses in your teaching. Your Minister of Education can help you with this.

3. Look into self-study materials that are available from your library or from a Christian publishing company. More and more videos and books are available for home study.

4. Decide if you flunked evaluation because of unchangeable personality traits or if you flunked because of bad habits that can be improved. Usually it's the latter.

5. If you have reason to suspect that your evaluator was prejudiced, you may want to ask for a reevaluation by someone else.

6. If, after all this, you still look like a "dud," you should consider working in some other area of the church or Sunday school. Perhaps you would be better as an assistant to another teacher, or you might like to help the superintendent with distribution of materials, attendance and offering records, and so forth.

Why and How to Be Funny

Why Be Funny?

Even young children have a sense of humor. By using humorous stories, you are teaching that it's good for Christians to laugh—that you don't have to be dull and bland in order to be spiritual.

Recent research suggests that teachers who use humor tend to get better test scores from their students. Using funny stories, or even funny test questions, alleviates anxiety and makes the learning process work better. People remember what makes them laugh.

It's been said that a laugh is the shortest distance between two people. When my wife and I received an unpleasant letter from the IRS, we were stunned. We knew we were in the right, but we dreaded the confrontation. Rather than "fight back," Sharon penned a humorous letter to the IRS. It worked—the matter was quickly cleared up, with good feelings all around.

Students relate to teachers who use humor. A distinguished, dignified preacher tells about moving from a sophisticated college-town church to an inner-city work. The inner-city church members did not accept him—until he began to tell funny stories. Then they warmed up to him.

How Can I Be Funny?

Bible stories can be full of humor when you imagine the feelings the characters may have experienced. Picture David standing before Goliath. What might he be thinking? Perhaps something like, "Whoa! What am I doing here when I could be home watching the war on television? If I don't connect with this first rock, I'm dog food."

Imagine Jezebel putting on her makeup. How long would it take her? What would she use? Imagine Lydia, the purple-seller, living in

Smile

Price, wear several rings, like a jewel merchant might have worn. Play with a ping-pong ball "pearl" as you speak, and bring on a white beach ball to represent the pearl of great price.

Children love it when a dignified adult puts himself into a story with exaggerated gestures and voices. It takes unselfconsciousness to talk with a squeaky voice or a growl, but it's well worth the sacrifice of your dignity. Vary the dynamics of your voice: talk slow, then fast, loud, then soft, and so forth.

Students enjoy being involved in a story. In the story of Jesus and His disciples in the storm on the Sea of Galilee, let the class make sound effects. Some can be "wind," some "thunder," and some "waves" or "screams." They won't soon forget the story.

One of the safest kinds of humor is the story you tell on yourself. When I tell my students how I shaved one whole side of my face before I realized the cap was still on my razor, they warm up to me in a hurry.

Practice noticing the funny side of life. Jot down humorous incidents so you won't forget them. Tell them to a friend to reinforce your memory, then use them in class when appropriate.

Can't think of anything funny?

Choose a good book of funny stories and jokes available at your Christian bookstore. Here are a few titles:

Church Chuckles II by James Weekley, CSS of Ohio, 1988

Good Clean Jokes for Kids by Bob Phillips, Harvest House, 1991

Mule Eggs & Topknots (two hundred twenty pages of humorous stories on a variety of topics) by King Duncan, Seven World's Press, 1986

Another Treasury of Clean Jokes by Tal D. Bonham, Broadman Press, 1983

a purple house with purple carpets and curtains, purple furniture, purple chariot, purple dog, purple jewelry, and purple clothes.

Try comparing Bible characters to modern counterparts. How would Solomon fare in the White House? Dressed in a double-breasted suit and wing tips? Where would he house his 1000 first ladies? What would the gossip sheets say about him? Or imagine the Prodigal Son in Las Vegas.

Simple props and gestures can make a humdrum story come to life. For example, when telling the parable of the Pearl of Great

1. Don't use stories that make fun of the handicapped.

2. Christian teachers should not have to be warned about using suggestive stories or stories full of gore. And yet we have all heard teachers and preachers tell such stories.

3. Don't mix Bible stories and fairy tales. Preface fictional stories with a disclaimer such as, "This is just a make-believe story. . . ."

4. Don't use satire or sarcasm with young children. They tend to take you literally. Either they will not get the point or they will get the wrong point.

5. Avoid too much detail when describing a sinful situation: a drunkard, an adulterer, or someone reading pornography. Don't be guilty of planting evil thoughts in young minds.

What If No One Laughs?

That's all right. If silence makes you uncomfortable, try adding something like, "Boy, when you have to explain your jokes, it's bad."

The best comedians have times when laughs come slowly, if at all. Students will still appreciate your attempts at humor; it shows you care about their feelings.

Chapter 10

Special Teaching Situations

Just like Sunday school, but totally different.

THIS BOOK HAS BEEN geared mainly to preparing Sunday school teachers. But I am well aware that these same teachers often participate in varied teaching experiences such as Vacation Bible School, camp, and home Bible studies. In this chapter we will suggest some ways to meet the unique opportunities and problems of these specialized ministries.

Vacation Bible School

If you are asked to teach in VBS, you should be aware of some of the differences between VBS and Sunday school. Although VBS formats have changed a great deal in recent years (A.M. programs, P.M. programs, one day a week programs, etc.), VBS continues to offer a concentrated approach to teaching.

1.   Expect larger classes in VBS, and the age-levels may meet in different rooms from their regular Sunday classrooms. The larger classes can make for noisy sessions and require more time to accomplish each task. Adequate helpers will be the key.

2.   VBS offers consecutive classes. This gives you an opportunity to do more review and reinforcement activities. You can tackle a week-long project, for example, in craft time or missions time.

3. VBS classes are more likely to be interrupted with special activities such as taking attendance, counting contest points, or serving refreshments.

4. VBS is an outreach opportunity because of the large number of unchurched children and youth who attend along with the members' children. VBS lessons tend to focus on faith-building themes such as the life of Christ. It is important to follow up on newcomers with phone calls or visits, because many of these newcomers may be won to the Lord later on.

5. VBS offers a chance for new teachers to try their hand for several days in a row. With a capable teacher as your assistant, you can learn fast in a school that meets five or ten days in a row.

6. Often informal methods are ideal for VBS because you have the children all morning or evening. You can take them outdoors for an activity or reinforce your lessons with a special class project that you wouldn't have time to complete in Sunday school.

Home Bible Study

Teaching in a small group is very different from teaching in a formal classroom setting. A small group leader seldom lectures for any length of time, because his role is more that of a coach than an informer. Here are some things to expect if you are asked to lead a home Bible study.

1. You need to prepare a flexible lesson. Seldom does a discussion go exactly the way the leader has planned it. A typical lesson might include giving some background material on the text, followed by a list of discussion questions. The group learns together rather than having a teacher tell them all they need to know.

2. The leader's job is to get the discussion going and keep it on track. He does this by preparing a good discussion guide, and then he plays the role of a good listener. If you are leading a group, your job is to get things started, keep track of time, encourage the shy, give praise, defuse arguments, stretch people's thinking, and summarize progress.

3. Expect all kinds of interruptions in a home setting. Children are a common sight in homes, and they interrupt at the most unpredictable times. Because most groups are evangelistic and contain non-Christians, you will occasionally hear a swear word or a request to smoke. You must develop a high tolerance for such things, yet not be afraid to have some standards for

behavior in the meetings. Other interruptions include: giant dogs, dozens of cats, persistent telephones, salesmen, televisions, and rest-room breaks.

4. The informal nature of small groups means that you will dress casually and take a low profile instead of being a stand-up, take-charge person.

It's important for you to be a good learner when leading a small group. Sit on the edge of your seat and lean forward. Listen visibly to your students and make appreciative comments like "uh huh," and "Yes, I can see that." If you do this well, your group will open up and share in the way that they should.

5. Be realistic in what you expect to accomplish in a small group. Most small groups are terminal, meeting for six to eight weeks at a time. Some of them will meet continuously, but most of them will begin to "fade" after a while unless you change topics or inject new life or new faces.

6. Home Bible studies don't always meet in homes. Sometimes they meet at the church building, but most of them prefer a neutral setting such as a home, an office building, or a restaurant.

7. Small groups also differ from Sunday school in their emphasis on worship. No matter what type of small group you are leading (Bible study, fellowship, action, or prayer) you will likely have a time of group prayer and/or singing. Often the leader will want to call for decisions for Christ to make the discussion turn to action.

8. Small groups tend to take on projects such as prayer projects, or special offerings, or even community cleanup projects. Some groups have a "money jar" that members contribute to each meeting and help themselves to when they are in a financial jam.

Christian Camp

Christian camps are life-changing institutions. Having a group of young people in a captive setting for a week, away from secular influences, tends to motivate and change young people in remarkable ways. However, most camp activities are informal and spirited rather than academic. Some camps have only a few classes offered, depending instead on special activities and speakers to educate their students.

Here are some of the problems you might face teaching in a camp.

I Remember VBS

Very Boring and Stupid

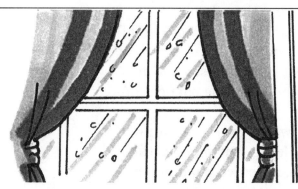

I poured my tired body into an easy chair and kicked off my shoes. "Done!" I announced to my wife. "I just turned in my grades and I am done teaching for another year."

"Hon, before I forget, Mae called and asked if you would teach the junior high class at VBS. I told her you would." She looked hopeful.

"What?!" I nearly screamed.

"Did I do wrong?" she asked, meekly.

"I was just about to say I just quit teaching and for mercy sakes don't sign me up for VBS this year."

She smiled her patient smile. Every Monday morning I quit teaching, so she wasn't alarmed. But I wasn't smiling. I was truly tired to the teeth of teaching. I was tired of Matthew, Mark, Luke, and John. Tired of lessons, devotions, talks. Tired of Cruden's and commentaries and quarterlies. Tired of students and schedules.

I still had three weeks to stew about VBS before it started. Sharon brought my materials home and I fanned through the quarterly. "The Beatitudes," the quarterly said. We are going to study the Beatitudes.

I stalled as long as I dared, but at last I had to think about the first lesson—tomorrow was the first day of VBS. I sat by the window watching the rain and feeling as gray as the sky. I was empty, bankrupt, utterly without human resources for the task.

"I have nothing to offer," I informed God. "Zero, busted, no spirit." The quarterly fell open to the first lesson and the text stared at me:

"Blessed are the poor in spirit: for theirs is the kingdom of heaven."

With blurry eyes I prayed, "Lord, I am poorest of spirit. Fill me with something for their sakes."

The first day of class went well, except for Randy. Randy was smaller than the other boys and seemed set on proving he was big. He fiddled with my overhead projector until he nearly knocked it over, bringing my blood to a gurgle. So I put him to work passing out papers, and tried to use his energy before he ran away with the class.

That evening the old feelings of fatigue and resentment were back. I had been out of college only three weeks and already it was back to lessons and deadlines and people and—I didn't open the quarterly that night. Just couldn't do it. Instead, I drove out into the country after supper till I came to a remote pasture on the Franklin's farm. There I walked around in grasses and wild flowers, thinking and praying until the sky was speckled with stars.

"Lord," I confessed, "I am so unlike you. My attitudes are not beautiful. How I wish I could be just like you."

It was five o'clock the next morning when I opened the quarterly and read:

"Blessed are they which do hunger and thirst after righteousness: for they shall be filled."

Randy found a new way to irritate me in class the next day. He tore up pieces of paper into odd shapes and laid them on the stage of my projector, creating weird shadows on the screen.

In the afternoon I climbed a tall, rubbery ladder and began to paint the house, a job I

had started the week before. Beneath me my younger daughter, Natalie, was playing softball in the yard with her friend, Cynthia. It was a hot, sticky day and I was not feeling very friendly.

"You girls be careful with that softball," I said with a growl. "I don't want you to hit the car or knock over my paint bucket, you understand?"

"We're being careful," Natalie replied with impatience in her voice.

"I mean it. If you hit something I'll put your head in this bucket of paint." Giggles. My sentence was followed by a crack of the bat and then a "kawhump!" Even from the top of the ladder I could see a nice round dent in the front fender of the car.

"We'll pay for it," Natalie mumbled with humility, as I studied the damage. I estimated the cost at about a hundred dollars but I kept it to myself.

"We're really sorry, Mr. Schantz," Cynthia added.

"This is so senseless, girls," I said, sternly. "Just a minute ago I told you to be careful."

"Are you mad at us?" Natalie asked.

" No, I'm not mad, I'm furious ! Now . . . just . . . go . . . get . . . out of the yard and . . . play . . . somewhere else. Please."

That evening I opened the quarterly and read the Scripture for the next lesson:

"Blessed are the merciful: for they shall obtain mercy."

Randy was not in class the next day and I was praising God for it until I realized what I was saying. Class was orderly for a change but a bit dull without him to keep me alert. I wondered if I had scared him away.

Wednesday afternoon. I had calmed down from yesterday's trouble, charmed by the bubble gum smell of the paint and sedated by the rhythmic swish of the brush as I spread rows of blue over the drab, thirsty siding.

Suddenly the front door flew open and my older daughter, Teresa, stomped out into the front yard, sobbing as she went.

"You get back in here, young lady," my wife hollered from the doorway where she stood red faced. I was shocked. Teresa, my sweet teenage daughter, who never gave us a moment of trouble, was fighting with her mother. Across the street Mr. Franks stopped mowing and gaped in disbelief. He was not a Christian but he knew we were. What must he be thinking?

Teresa's best friend, Lori, arrived at that moment, just in time to catch the drama.

"Lori," I said somberly, "maybe you had better go on home."

I don't remember climbing down the ladder, but soon I was standing in the living room in my filthy jeans, my face speckled with blue paint, trying to reconcile mother and daughter.

The lesson for the next day was:

"Blessed are the peacemakers: for they shall be called the children of God."

On Thursday Randy pulled out all the stops. He talked, dropped things, entertained the girls, and faked coughing fits. Finally I had had it. "Randy!" I was shouting. I was hot. "That's it! That's all! I want no more of it!" The class froze from embarrassment and Randy meekly settled down.

By now it was clear to me that God intended this VBS to teach me a new set of attitudes. I was learning, slowly, and I had peeked ahead to see the last lesson. It was about persecution.

"Blessed are they which are persecuted for righteousness' sake: for theirs is the kingdom of heaven."

I had been persecuted all week by Randy, but where was the blessedness?

Friday was different. Randy seemed subdued, almost sad. He even asked a question, a serious, sincere question, and I nearly broke my jaws trying to answer it. But as we walked to the auditorium for the closing session, he came up alongside me and said, "I know what VBS stands for. It stands for very boring and stupid, like you."

I tried to smile, hoping he was just teasing, but he seemed serious. The remark didn't anger me, but it hurt. Perhaps he was right. I had not done my best teaching this week. Because of my poor attitude I was "driving with the brakes on."

Soon VBS was all over, except for the closing program. I had Saturday and Sunday to reflect on the week. I had certainly learned a lot from the week's unusual events. I wasn't sure what I had learned from Randy. Who needs a Randy? Where is the glory in persecution?

When the closing program was over Sunday night, I hurried out to the car. I had done my duty for another year and I was almost to the car when someone grabbed my arm. It was Randy's mother. Her eyes sparkled as she spoke.

"I just want you to know how much you have done for Randy," she said. "It's the first time he has ever shown any interest in the Bible. He was fascinated by your overhead projector and told me all about it. He can say all the Beatitudes and he wants me to buy him a new Bible. He was so overwhelmed by all the attention he got from the other kids. See, he doesn't have many friends and, well, he just had a wonderful time. This morning he said to me, 'If Mr. Schantz is still teaching in Bible college when I grow up, I'm going to Bible college.'"

I was stunned. I mumbled a "Thank you" and headed for the car to wait for the others. I just sat there thinking. Perhaps, I decided, God does not need terrific teachers, just willing ones. Maybe he can use even very boring and stupid servants for his glory.

1. Weather. Many classes are held outdoors or under an open pavilion. The wind can play games with your notes and visuals. The sun gets very warm. And right in the middle of your most important point, the maintenance man starts riding his lawn mower tractor around and around your class!

When the nights are cool, the mosquitoes turn into vampires.

Storms come up that are not on the schedule. I once spoke at a camp assembly in a large metal building with a metal roof. A storm came up just as I began, and although I shouted through my speech, I discovered later that no one heard a word I had said. I gave the world's longest pantomime!

2. Competing attractions. There are lots of *fun and interesting* things at camps. Like faculty members swimming nearby; lake waves rolling in and speedboats roaring by; a raccoon that's locked in the kitchen; practical jokes that get out of hand; sports activities that go overtime and steal your class time.

A teacher must prepare well for lessons that can compete with all these temptations. And don't forget mosquito repellent.

3. Working conditions. I once spoke in a camp pavilion that was situated next to a busy road. Cars, trucks, and tractors got far more attention than my speech. The building was lighted by only one or two hanging light bulbs. I had designed my talk with lots of visuals, and no one could see them. In such settings, turn the students so they face away from the road, and give them handouts that they can easily read.

Watch out for special glitches. Speaking at campfire can be a problem. The fire dies down and you can't see your notes. Mosquitoes as big as birds attack your nose during your talk. Your pants leg catches on fire and you don't know it!

If you are scheduled to teach in camp, get to the camp early and look over the situation. Try to anticipate bottlenecks and problems such as a classroom with no windows and poor lights, or a class that is scheduled right before lunch. (Serve pretzels to tide them over!) Take along plenty of Plasti-Tak, transparent tape, and thumbtacks. Throw in a couple bright light bulbs and an extension cord or two. Pack plenty of big, bold markers and extra chalk.

Christian School

The rapid rise of Christian elementary and secondary schools has created a need for trained Christian teachers. If you enjoy teaching Sunday school, or if you are a public school teacher dissatisfied with secular education, you might well enjoy teaching in a Christian school. Here are some things to expect.

1. Christian schools differ greatly from each other. Some are an imitation of the old one-room schools—a kind of all-day study hall with kids working in workbooks and teachers and volunteers giving over-the-shoulder help. Others are copies of the traditional schools that today's middle-agers remember: disciplined, content-centered, serious. Still others are carbon copies of the local public schools with a Christian emphasis added to the curriculum and activities.

2. The trend is toward hiring certified teachers and teachers with master's degrees in order to legitimize the school in the eyes of the state and to provide a higher level of instruction. Salaries are not outstanding, as a rule, so teachers must be dedicated to sacrifice and stewardship.

3. Most Christian schools are tightly structured. Creative experimentation is discouraged. In some cases, daily lesson plans are already planned out for teachers. Record-keeping is very important. Discipline is a major emphasis and is demanded as an expression of Christian character. Many schools require students to wear uniforms or follow a certain dress code. All teachers and students follow a handbook.

4. Christian schools recognize the role of parents in education, and they require teachers to work closely with parents. Parents often work as volunteers in the classroom, for example, and teacher-parent conferences are frequent.

5. Christian schools attempt to permeate all subject matter with Christian references. Science, for example, is taught from a creationist viewpoint. History includes the religious history of our country. Evangelism is practiced in the schools, since many of them admit non-Christians as long as they agree to abide by the rules.

Those who teach in Christian schools report a high degree of satisfaction but admit to high demands and low salary as problems.

Home Schooling

The fastest growing branch of Christian schooling is home schooling. Home schooling is not a new phenomenon, although the tremendous interest in it is new. It is legal in all states, but laws governing its practice differ from state to state. Home schooling is partly a reaction to public school failures—public schools that don't teach godly values and academic skills, and schools that do teach humanistic values and provide negative socialization.

Home schoolers believe, as many educators believe, that young children in particular profit more from personal attention than from formal classroom settings. They home school to protect their children from public school's so-called "socialization" such as swearing, sex, and violence. They home school to assure that their children learn with close personal attention and adequate homework. And they home school so that they can instill Christian values in their children *before* they have to face the worldly values of public schools and daily life.

There are several approaches to home schooling. Three of the more popular motifs are:

1.   Holding children back from public school for the first couple of years to teach them the basics at home.

2.   Teaching children at home all the way through elementary and even secondary education levels.

3.   Teaching at home but enrolling children in a nearby Christian school for testing, social activities, field trips, and recreational activities.

Home schoolers take their job seriously. Here are some of their typical practices:

- Setting up a room of the house like a schoolroom—complete with desks, chalkboard, computer, study carrel, etc.
- Spending a specific number of hours each day formally instructing their child, and counting him absent if he is sick. They follow a schedule and supervise homework.
- Keeping careful records of students' achievement, in case their schooling is ever questioned, and to help them adjust if they ever go back into a public school situation. Some home schoolers even videotape their children's verbal reading skills for visual proof of progress.
- Following a quality Christian curriculum or even using public school textbooks for the sake of equivalency.

- Working hard to provide their children with socialization, through church activities, neighborhood friendships, and community field trips, then documenting this socialization with records.

If you decide to home school your children, you should consider doing the following:

1. Read some of the many books and magazines available on the subject of home schooling. Some areas of the country even have bookstores for home schoolers where you can purchase curriculum, materials, and aids over the counter. Attend a home schoolers convention in your area. Visit a family that is home schooling and see how it's done.

2. Check the laws of your state, and then inform your local education authorities of your intention to home school. Develop a good relationship with them, and be ready to provide them with your plan and objectives.

3. Expect to make a substantial commitment of time and energy to be a home school teacher. Financial outlay is not significant as a rule, but the cost in time and concentration is substantial. It's difficult to maintain a home, answer the phone, and handle other interruptions while trying to home school your children.

Be aware that home schooling is controversial. The most serious objections seem to be:

a. Socialization. Some parents feel that their children must be around large groups of their own age in order to be properly socialized. Well-known educators debate this. Meanwhile, home schoolers are quietly proving that their children can be socialized in the community, and, in fact, may be better socialized because they see that their children meet a variety of age groups in more settings than just a classroom or sports playing field.

b. Unqualified parents. Parents without certification or master's degrees are accused of being unfit for home schooling. Home schoolers argue that young children need personal attention more than classroom management skills or a high level of education.

c. Truancy. Well-meaning friends and nosy neighbors sometimes regard home schooled children as school-skippers. Church members are often the worst critics of home schoolers, when they should probably be the best supporters.

d. Commitment. To teach your own child requires a level of dedication and sacrifice not commonly known among parents. But most home schoolers are studied and know what they are getting into. They are ready to make the commitment.

Public School

There are many Christians in America who are involved in the public school system as teachers or administrators. Their influence is considerable. The James Dobson video, *Molder of Dreams,* is a stimulating presentation of a Christian in a public school classroom making a significant difference. It's the story of a Christian teacher who was honored by Ronald Reagan as Teacher of the Year.

Christian public school teachers actually have certain freedoms to witness to their faith. They can teach the Bible as literature. They can carry a Bible with them. They can witness in the hallways. They can answer questions about their faith. For a more detailed discussion of these freedoms, see *Christ in the Classroom,* by Arnold Burron and John Eidsmoe, or *Faith at the Blackboard* by Brian Hill (see Resources).

Of course a teacher's daily Christian walk is likely in itself to influence children for good. A Christian teacher models clean speech, dedication to teaching, honesty and integrity, compassion, and love for students.

Chapter 11

Emotions, Who Needs Them?

If I'm such a good teacher, why do I feel so bad?

THE INTENSE EMOTIONS that teachers sometimes feel have their purpose. Emotions may be painful, but a teacher without feelings will not be a very good teacher. The challenge is for a teacher to experience the full range of emotions but to let them fire him into better performance rather than defeat. Let's take a look at some of the more common and troubling emotions teachers face.

Feelings of Failure

Teachers who feel like a failure are probably basing their feelings on circumstantial evidence rather than the truth. For example, some teachers put too much stock in visual feedback from students. If one student falls asleep in class, the teacher goes home saying to himself, "I must be a boring teacher." The truth is probably that his soporific student was up until 3:00 A.M. playing video games, or he's taking antihistamines for his allergies, or he is simply a very dull person who can't appreciate a genius. Don't blame yourself if you don't know for sure. If a certain student is frequently absent, the teacher may say to himself, "If I were a better teacher, I would have perfect attendance from my pupils." But this is unrealistic. Did this teacher attend every class when he was in school? Probably not. The point is that students are responsible for their behavior, not you. You are responsible to do the best you can. Students are responsible to be there faithfully, on time, and awake. This is not to say that you can ignore all careless behavior. It's just that a teacher must not assume all responsibility for it. Find out why the student is absent if you can. Talk to the "sleeper" about his Saturday night habits, and maybe speak to his parents to get their support.

The most common cause of failure feelings is the setting of impossible standards for oneself and for students. Teaching is not like painting a masterpiece with every brush stroke and shade in perfect blend. It's more like finger painting with frequent painting over and rubbing out. This is true because when you are dealing with a group of students, there are too many variables. Nothing ever goes according to your plan when you are dealing with humans. They don't always cooperate, because they have freedom of will. So ease off on yourself. Get off your case. Stop beating yourself bloody because your class work doesn't measure up to some Disneyland ideal of teaching.

And don't expect too much from students. After all, that's why they are students—to learn and grow, not to demonstrate their perfection. It's been said that "teachers should not expect adult behavior out of anyone *less* than forty years of age." I would add, "Don't expect adult behavior out of anyone *over* forty either!" Adults can be some of the worst offenders in the classroom—talking out loud, coming in late, arguing, joking too much, and more.

Perhaps the media deserves some blame for teachers' feelings of failure. Multimillion-dollar talk shows and stand-up comedians create the impression that speakers can be eternal entertainers. It isn't so. Few of us will ever have the kind of talent that is displayed on the networks, or be rewarded so handsomely with praise and money. There are probably 10,000 ordinary teachers for every teacher who is truly exceptional. Professor William Lyon Phelps once remarked that the only way a teacher can get national attention is to spit on the flag, steal from the treasury, or run off with the principal. Unless you're willing to try one of those options, be prepared to be ordinary.

One of the greatest compliments I ever received on my teaching came from a former student of mine when I was visiting in her home. She said, "Do you know what I appreciated most about you when I was a student in your classes?"

"No," I shrugged, wondering if she would comment on my methods, or my vocabulary, or what.

"The thing I most appreciated is how ordinary you were. You were not above us. You had moods and frustrations and problems. I found school difficult, and when I saw that you, too, were struggling, it inspired me not to quit."

What can a teacher do if he is wrestling with feelings of failure? Here are some suggestions:

Try to distinguish facts from feelings. Analyze your work, perhaps using the evaluation forms in Chapter 9. Make a list of the things you are doing right—even little things like being on time and having a strong voice. If you find you really are failing, make an effort to improve. If you decide you are merely *feeling* like a failure, then get some help from a good friend or an experienced teacher.

Get the big picture. As a teacher you are part of a team of workers in the church. Your students have more than you to help them grow in Christ. They have parents, a minister, elders, deacons, and other teachers. No one expects you to carry the whole load of hay, so don't expect it of yourself.

Consider the limitations of your students. Sunday school, after all, is a volunteer school. Anyone can attend regardless of ability, background, or level of maturity. Some years you may get a whole class of "black sheep" whose only ability is to "baaa" everything you try to do. You can't make a swan out of a sparrow, and you cannot single-handedly transform limited students into intellectual and spiritual giants.

As a teacher in a Christian college for twenty-five years, I have had one or more of every kind. Some of my students can barely read the back of a cereal box. Some of them come to college not knowing the difference between Noah and a Teenage Mutant Ninja Turtle. Most of my students are average, a few are truly brilliant, and there's always a lunatic fringe. No matter how hard I work and pray, I cannot raise the IQ level of my students nor make up for years of failure in their past.

Let Jesus be the Messiah. You are not a savior to your students, but rather a friend and teacher. Ask God to help you teach—then believe that he will, and turn the class over to him when you are done with it.

Jesus himself had many "failures." When his ministry was at its peak, the crowds abandoned him, students denied him, and his own family was embarrassed about him. Are you and I somehow superior to Jesus that no one will ever dislike us or reject our teaching?

Take care of your body. Teaching is extra hard, even impossible, when you allow yourself to become physically run down. Get sleep. Take walks. Trim your schedule. Eat right. Your students may stay up all night and eat like a hippo, but teachers can't afford to be out of shape.

Feeling Afraid

Stage fright is standard fare for anyone in the speaking business, and that's not all bad. There is some evidence that teachers who have absolutely no feelings of nervousness are bores! Nerves show that you are alive and sensitive and aware of the importance of your task.

Feelings of fear are probably most common among very intelligent, creative thinkers who imagine the worst, and among the inexperienced who don't know what to expect. They fear the unknown.

If you are hesitant to teach, you are in the company of the greatest characters in the Bible. Jonah ran away from his class and had to be dragged back by a sea monster. Moses rattled off a list of excuses. Jeremiah begged off saying, "I am but a child." Timothy had stomach troubles, and the apostle Paul spoke with "weakness and fear."

Just what scares you may differ from what frightens another teacher. Some teachers fear being laughed at. Others fear making a mistake or being challenged by a student. Some fear they will blank out, or get sick, or say something truly stupid. Some are afraid of boring students.

The trick to handling fear is to make it work for you. Fear can even be exciting. That's why we pay big money at theme parks to go on monster roller coasters and through dark tunnels and high in the sky on Ferris wheels. How much fun would a theme park be without the terror?

What can you do to deal with your fears? Here are some suggestions:

Be scared at home. The time to be afraid is when you are preparing your lesson. Let fear motivate you to be as prepared as possible, then in the classroom you will be calm. Write a good lesson plan. Have your visuals and activities ready to go. Practice your talk. Get to church early. Set up your classroom and greet the early arrivals. Preparation soothes the spirit.

Express, don't impress. Teaching becomes scary when we teachers try to make a good impression instead of simply expressing God's Word in a simple way. As a college professor I have watched many young teachers and preachers practice their first talks on an audience. I can always tell when one of them is about to fall on his face. It's when they try to impress the audience by using big words, or by speaking without notes, or by imitating some fabulous speaker they heard at a convention.

Don't run from it. No matter how scared you may feel, you will never overcome your fears by running away from the task. Professor William James used to say something like, "We do not run away because we are afraid; rather, we are afraid because we are running away." Keep going back to class until you begin to feel more confident. It takes time to learn to teach and time for students to relax around you enough to make your task fun instead of terror-filled.

Use a method that takes the focus off of you. It has been said that Socrates used the question and answer method because he was so ugly that he didn't want anyone looking at him lecture!

Certain teaching methods do take the focus off of you and also provide physical movement that helps you relax. Learning centers, for example, take quite a bit of preparation, but in class your role is merely a supporting role rather than a visible role.

Discussion method passes the attention around to the whole class. If you do it right, you only have to get it started and help steer it in the right direction.

Using visuals, videotapes, and audiotapes for a portion of your class hour will give you a break from the "starring role."

Learn to love butterflies. No matter how well you prepare and no matter what techniques you use, you may always have trouble with butterflies in your stomach. Learn to accept them. Talk to them. "Hi, butterflies. How are you, my friends? Look at how my hands are shaking today. I must be alive—I'm moving. Boy, is my heart racing. That's good. It will give me energy. My face sure feels hot. It's good for my complexion."

Learn not to be afraid of being afraid.

Keep it all in perspective. One class is not going to make or break you or your students. You are not so important that you need to be perfect.

I once interviewed an elderly woman who had spent her life teaching in difficult New York schools. "What's the secret of surviving the classroom?" I asked. Without hesitation she fired back, "Don't take yourself or your task too seriously."

Good advice for the tense.

Feelings of Ignorance

You might think that a teacher would feel really smart, but it's not so. All my teaching career I have wrestled with feelings of ignorance, and I know other teachers who feel the same way. Perhaps the feeling has a purpose—perhaps it keeps us from being overconfident or from neglecting preparation. Even so, it's not a comfortable feeling, and it must be kept under control or a teacher will get discouraged.

What causes this feeling? Here are some ideas:

The information explosion has generated a lot of insecurity in us. We begin to feel that we don't know enough or that we need to be using newer, fancier methods and equipment.

Fortunately, some things never change. "Jesus Christ is the same yesterday and today and forever" (Hebrews 13:8). Christian teachers are dealing with unchanging truths. Sin will always be wrong. Godliness will always be right. This comforting fact is unique in a world that's constantly reversing its judgments and constantly experimenting with truth.

Yes, methods do change, but often they are only new versions of old methods. There's only so much you can do with materials and information and students. *Newer* doesn't automatically mean *better.* Indeed, as the rate of change increases, so does our need for stability. Old tried and true methods may do just fine in many cases. I am writing this book with a yellow wooden pencil on paper. Next I will type it on a typewriter. I've written about twenty books and numerous articles this way—more than some of my friends who have computers with laser printers. I've read that James Michener has written all of his king-sized novels on a manual typewriter. The method is only a means.

Ben Franklin's advice is appropriate here: "Be not the first to try the new, nor the last to give up the old."

Students can make you feel ignorant. There's an old saying that "any fool can ask more questions than all the wise men in the world can answer." Students are very talented at playing on a teacher's insecurities. They know how to make you feel dumb.

Teachers must resist the temptation to feel they must know all things about all subjects—it's impossible, and to try to pull it off is to invite disaster. Students can tell a "snow job" from miles away. Far better to say, "I don't know. Let me check on that," than to feign omniscience.

How should you deal with feelings of ignorance?

Don't claim to know more than you do. Indeed, by taking a humble stance, you may very well enhance your teaching. I have found that my students really warm up to me when I admit my ignorance and ask for help. I ask them for advice. I ask their opinions. I ask them for information.

"What's the name of that rock band that keeps having riots?"

"Does this tie look OK with this suit?"

"How do you guys feel about school reforms?"

This kind of admission helps students feel needed and less likely to "attack you" because you do not claim to be a know-it-all.

Don't answer all their questions. Students ask questions for many reasons besides wanting answers. Sometimes they ask questions to get you off the track. "What team are you behind in the World Series?" for example. Sometimes they ask questions to show how smart they are. "Did you know that you can change computer chips in your car to hop it up?" And sometimes they ask good questions that are simply not answered fully in the Bible. "How come my baby brother was born blind?"

Jesus, who knew all things, did not give a factual answer to all questions. Sometimes he reversed the question (Luke 10:25, 26). Sometimes he answered a question with a question or with a story (Luke 12:41, 42; Luke 10:29). Sometimes he delayed his answer (Luke 7:19-22). And sometimes he asked the motive behind the question (Luke 20:23, 24) or even disregarded the question altogether (Luke 20:7, 8).

Let feelings of ignorance drive you to study and prepare. Let those feelings keep you humble and teachable. Let them cause you to seek God's help in your task. Reverse some of those questions and become a better teacher.

Feelings of Anger

Of all the feelings that teachers have, anger is one of the more common and one that's most often denied. After all, we tend to feel guilty about feeling angry, as if anger were a terrible sin. If it is, then Jesus was a sinner, for he got angry on several occasions, and it showed!

We are taught in the Scriptures not to be angry without a cause, not to get angry quickly, not to let our anger linger, and not to express our anger in violence or swearing. But to deny anger or repress it is an invitation to ulcers and high blood pressure, among other things.

What causes teachers to get angry?

1. Fatigue. When teachers come to class worn out emotionally and physically, the slightest provocation will touch them off. You can be sure that in an hour's time something will happen to touch your anger button at least once. If you are tired, you risk an explosion.

2. Worries. Teachers who are burdened with family problems, job problems, and financial worries are teachers who are easily offended. They will see slights and insults that aren't really there. They will be impatient with behavior that is perfectly normal for children.

3. Impossible standards. When a teacher has perfectionist standards for his students or for himself, he will be under a constant strain to do better. That kind of pressure is exhausting and leads to eruptions and burnout.

4. Student behavior that threatens a teacher's self image. In his book, *Teaching With Feeling*, Herbert Greenburg suggests that a common cause of teacher anger is that a student's behavior reminds a teacher of her own weakness. For example, a clinging student might remind a teacher of her own tendency to be over-dependent on her husband. A restless student might remind a teacher of her own impatience.

5. Accumulated irritations. Probably the most common trigger of anger in the classroom is the pile-up of little irritations to a point that the teacher loses self-control. Two students are tardy. One is doodling. Another is looking out the window. The pencil sharpener broke. A picture fell off the wall. A page is missing from your notes. And suddenly the door opens and another student arrives fifteen minutes late! BOOM! BOOM! The storm breaks in a fury of angry words.

What can teachers do about angry feelings?

Good planning and preparation can help a teacher avoid accumulated irritations. Be sure you have adequate materials so students don't fight over them. Check out the pencil sharpener and the rest of the room. Talk to students about the importance of being on time and how to come in quietly if they have to be late. Get to bed early on Saturday night so you are rested for class. Resolve problems at home so they don't spill over into the classroom.

When you get angry, admit it. Say something like, "Bobby, will you and Judy turn around and look this way? I feel bad when you don't listen." Using an "I-message" lets the class know that their behavior is being noticed, and that you are a person who has feelings—not a wooden statue. These I-messages do not focus on what the student did, but rather on how it makes you the teacher feel. It's a way of absorbing some of the embarrassment of being caught angry.

Sometimes you can admit the anger later when you have calmed down. "Last Sunday I was very upset with the way the back row talked all through the lesson. I try hard to prepare a good lesson, and it hurts my feelings when no one listens."

Students learn much about you and Christian living by the way you handle anger. But they will not learn if you and I are determined to deny that we are ever angry.

After class, go to any student who has angered you and tell him about it. Seek his support or forgiveness. This is the biblical way.

There are many other techniques teachers develop on their own for coping with anger: humor, leaving the room for a moment, having a private cry, or even calling for help.

No matter what method you use to manage your feelings of anger, there will come a day when you "lose it." You will verbally lash out at someone and probably say things you shouldn't or things that are exaggerated. The important thing is not to throw things or hurt anyone, but to carry on with the class. Later, when you and they have calmed down, you may want to issue an apology and explanation. This is not "crawling." It is Christian to say, "I'm sorry. I lost my temper back there. It's not my way to chew people out in public. I want you all to remember that I love you, and I'm trying to help you grow up. Be patient with me; I'm just a human being."

If you find yourself exploding frequently, it's a danger signal. You need to seek support from a friend or even professional help in some cases. It may be an indication that you simply do not have the emotional strength and stability needed to be a classroom teacher.

All in all, anger is a form of caring. It's a kind of concentrated energy that can work to make you a better teacher or a worse one, depending on whether you admit it and use it, or hide it and suffer for it.

Feelings of Frustration

One of the greatest myths of all time is that teachers are always supposed to be calm, cool, and collected. Somehow the Christian classroom is supposed to resemble a worship service rather than a learning factory.

And yet is there any kind of work that goes without frustration and disorder? Have you ever cooked a meal that didn't have glitches? Have you ever worked on a car without banging your knuckles? Have you ever papered a room without a few wrinkles? Or cleaned a drain without spilling water on the floor?

The momentous task of teaching with its many details and cantankerous people is going to be frustrating. Some days you will feel like you are being nibbled to death by a million minnows. Some typical frustrations include:

1. Time problems. Some days you are through with the lesson early, and you have to fill time until the bell rings. Other days you don't get past the first point, and the bell rings.

2. Student differences. One student is finished with his workbook in five minutes. The others are still on the first question.

3. Disappearing parts. One piece is missing from the puzzle your beginners are working on. A page of your notes has vanished. One of your primary students has disappeared, and no one seems to have a clue where she is.

4. Interruptions. The Sunday school superintendent interrupts to make an announcement—for the third time. Little Albert has to "go potty" right now or else, and he just went five minutes ago.

5. Slow movers. It has taken you fifteen minutes of class time to get all of your students seated on the story rug and quieted down.

Who wouldn't be frustrated?

Other than throwing things or kicking the dog, what can a teacher do about feelings of frustration?

Get more help. You may need someone to help you in class with management of children or to display visuals. You are carrying a Chinese load if you try to do it all yourself. Perhaps someone could share your lecture—you teach ten minutes, then let someone else teach. Invite a guest speaker once a month. Ask for parents to serve as volunteers with reading time. Let your teenage children help you make up your crafts. Divide your task and conquer it.

Reduce the size of your task. Perhaps you need to split your class and reduce the size of it by half. Maybe you ought to just eliminate some of the activities that have only frustrated you—don't use the workbooks, save crafts for one Sunday a month, eliminate or modify refreshments.

When you have cut the task down to size, you can "spread out" a little and have breathing room. And never put off until tomorrow what you can *eliminate* altogether.

Invest in adequate materials. Replace those aging puzzles with the missing pieces. Get a larger box of crayons and more pencils. Fix or replace the broken pencil sharpener. Order extra workbooks for visitors.

Where do you find the money? Take up a special offering. Put your needs on the bulletin board or in the church paper. Do a class project to earn money. Borrow from your Christmas fund. Print some money in the basement—*just kidding!*

Lengthen your class. Hold an extended session that starts a half hour early or remains later. Use this time for enrichment activities.

Learn to like frustration. Start writing a book on *How I Survived a Thousand and Two Frustrations in a Kindergarten Classroom.* You could get rich!

What Can I Do? Where Can I Hide?

One of my greatest fears as a teacher is that someone will stand up in class and confront me, trying to make a fool out of me.

I'm routinely teaching a typical middle-age class, made up of lawyers, Wall Street barons, computer technicians, rocket scientists, and former U.S. Presidents.

Suddenly one of them stands up and says, "You don't know what you are talking about. You couldn't be more wrong if you had a college degree in 'How to Make Mistakes.' This is the stupidest Sunday school class I've ever seen. Why don't you go work in the nursery department where you belong?"

The blood drains from my face and I begin to blink rapidly. Nausea wells up in me and I grow dizzy. Before I know what's happened, I drop to the floor in a dead faint.

When students see how easily I fluster, they make it the goal of their lives to assault my ignorance in public.

One of them brings long lists of impossible questions for me to answer.

"In 25 words or less explain the phrase, 'baptized for the dead' in 1 Corinthians 15:29."

"Well, I uh . . . ."

"How many verses are in Isaiah?"

"Isaiah? That's in the New Testament, isn't it?"

The class roars with pleasure at my stupidity. Attendance climbs because they bring their friends to watch me stammer and faint.

Meanwhile a journalist in the class has been busy checking my credentials. Right in the middle of my lecture he stands up and addresses the class.

"I've been doing a little checking around, and I've learned from reliable sources that our so-called teacher here actually got thirteen Cs, nine Ds, and five Fs on his high school record, and he never graduated. Furthermore, his IQ is lower than his age, and the only thing he ever reads is TV Guide."

He sits down amid applause and laughter, and a lawyer jumps up.

"How's your bank account?" he challenges me, "because you made seven libelous statements in one lecture."

A computer whiz joins him with a long sheet of paper in hand. "I've analyzed your last 10 lessons, and here's a printout of your mistakes:

"1.   You said 'uh' 982 times."

"2.   You misquoted four Bible verses."

"3.   Your statistics were off by an average of 12 percent."

"4.   You mispronounced the name of every major Bible character."

178   By this time I've started seeing my counselor three times a week. I begin to lose weight and I can't sleep. I roam around the house at night, trying to memorize encyclopedias and dictionaries.

Soon I have to have a security escort to class. Then one day everything falls apart, and students begin throwing books and purses at me. I break down and resign the class in shame.

Next Sunday I go before the congregation and make a public confession. "Yes, I am an impostor; I admit it, but I promise to get help."

With that confession I move down to the nursery department, where I serve the rest of my days changing diapers and recycling them.

Now that you know what it's like to be confronted, here are some things to remember:

1. Truly educated students will be your best friends. They will never make you feel small or ignorant. They realize that they, too, have large areas of ignorance in their lives. They don't expect you to know everything about every subject, not even everything about the Bible lesson.

2. Angry, rude people are often people with personal problems unrelated to you or your class. Befriend them outside of class and they may become more supportive.

3. If someone does yell at you, remember Solomon's advice: "A soft answer turns away wrath."

4. If you make a mistake, admit it. Don't try to hide it. Students respect teachers who admit their limitations.

5. If you run into a serious confrontation with a student, seek the assistance of the local leadership. Don't try to go it alone.

6. Working in the nursery isn't so bad, if you don't mind the odor.

Chapter 12

The Creative Teacher

*There ought to be a better way to do this.
Rhonda is so creative with her kindergartners.
I've just got to try something different.*

SOONER OR LATER it hits all teachers—the realization that they are bored with their task, or frustrated with methods that don't seem to work well any more.

Enter creativity.

Why Be Creative?

It's godlike to create. God is creative, and we are made in his image. One of his favorite words is *new—new* mercies, *new* creation, *new* life, *new* Heaven and earth. Jesus was the most creative man who ever lived. No one was ever bored with him. They loved him, or they hated him, or they were puzzled by him, but never bored. The Bible is the most creative book ever printed. It's imaginative, stimulating. It's *alive!*

Being creative is not an option for Christians. It's part of our spiritual growth to keep changing, stretching, reaching for newness. Your creative spirit is a wonderful example to your students. When your spirit is dull or commonplace, you are a poor example to students.

Your students are creative. If you want to "match minds" with students, you have to get on their channel. Watch them at work—so busy, so daring, so uninhibited. Learn to play the way

179

they do, and you will find yourself thinking in new patterns. You will become a student again, and you will be able to speak the language of the student.

Creativity resurrects. Monotony and routine are death to a teacher. Far better to try something wild and crazy than to die of safety. If your lessons are perfectly normal and perfectly respectable, they are probably also perfectly dull.

Creativity puts the fun back in teaching. It makes teaching an art instead of a serious science or a dry duty.

Creativity reduces anxiety. Tension builds in us when we think there is only one way to go. Alternatives give us breathing room. And there are always alternatives when it comes to methods and approaches to teaching. There are no commandments carved in stone when it comes to styles of teaching.

Being creative makes better use of time and energy. "Wisdom is better than strength," said Solomon (Ecclesiastes 9:16), and he should know. Some teachers just work harder and harder and harder until they have a breakdown or burn out and quit. Better to work smarter, not harder.

Caution: Creativity is a valuable human skill, but it's not a savior. Other types of thinking are also important: logic, IQ, memory, judgment. Indeed, the most effective creative thinkers are those who also have the savvy to carry out their ideas with common sense.

Get an Attitude

All human beings are creative, but some are more creative than others. True, it's partly a gift, but more often than not the extra-creative teacher is simply one with a set of attitudes that make for creativity.

Develop an attitude of appreciation. If you want to be creative, begin by taking a fresh look at what you have to work with. Creative teachers see beauty and potential where others see only problems.

Take students, for example. Is your class too small? Rather than bemoan its size, decide to make it the best small class in the world. Chances are that if you do, it will grow. A noted scientist who was semiretired advertised for students part time. He wanted to share with the younger generation what he had learned on his way to a Nobel prize. Only two students showed interest, but this did not discourage the scientist. Every day he drove forty miles to teach his two students. A few years later, both of those students won Nobel prizes themselves.

H. L. Mencken once said, "Love is the triumph of imagination over intelligence." Can you see your students with an imaginative eye? Those two boys who love to fight—perhaps they are debaters in the making. Put their skills to work. And the girl who constantly doodles—maybe she is a budding artist or a future writer of Christian books. Get acquainted with her doodling skills, and put them to work. Every class has a clown—maybe that clown needs a way to express his creative energy in a role play, drama, or some other way.

Appreciate your students. One day one of them will replace you. How well he does as a teacher will depend partly on the encouragement he receives from you.

Appreciate yourself. Teachers tend to cannibalize themselves with criticism and second-guessing. Resist it. Are you a quiet person? Don't resent it. Choose teaching methods that emphasize your listening skills: discussion, projects, visuals, counseling. Turn your weakness into a strength. If you are old, fat, and ugly, dress up as a bag lady and teach a lesson on respect for the homeless—*just kidding!* Instead of groaning about your looks, dress up like a queen and make the best of the body you have. After all, nine-tenths of what shows in a person is clothing—only the face and arms and legs are visible.

Appreciate your facilities. Don't have nice chairs for your classroom? Take them out and use carpet samples to hold "Chinese" Sunday school. Is your room dark and gloomy? Let students paint the walls white, then let them paint on murals or brightly colored flowers. Maybe keep the darkness and make it special. Use candles like a fine restaurant does to create a mood. Or turn off all the lights and hold a catacombs lesson on persecution.

Henry Ford said, "When you can do the ordinary in an extraordinary way, you will command the attention of the world." What could you, a teacher, do with roll call, take-home papers, a simple chalkboard, the U.S. mail, quarterlies and workbooks, average students, rest-room breaks, and Bible stories? You could do a lot if you appreciate what you have.

Be daring. One reason children are so creative is that they are willing to try things. Their need for adventure is greater than their need for security and peer approval. Think about how you learned as a child. You learned to write by filling pages and pages with scribbles. You learned to draw by doodling. You learned to ride a bike and roller skate by falling down. You learned to climb trees by trying to climb trees. You learned to talk by making strange sounds.

Somewhere on the way to adulthood we lose that spirit of risk and choose to be safe instead. In choosing safety, we have often chosen boredom and ineffectiveness.

What could you do as a teacher to "stick your neck out"? One teacher I read about decided to build a Noah's ark and stock it with real animals. It didn't turn out exactly the way he planned, but it made the newspapers, and it's something his class will never forget.

Here are some daring ideas to get you started thinking in creative channels:

- One week a month let one of your students teach the class.
- Take your students to a mission field, and let them serve truly needy people.
- Recruit new students until your class of 10 numbers 110.
- Give each student $10 and ask each to double it for missions.
- Make your classroom the most beautiful room in the world.
- Invite the mayor to visit your class and talk about civic duty.
- Ask your class to memorize the entire book of Proverbs.
- Dress up like Jesus and teach the Sermon on the Mount on a nearby hill.
- Teach the lesson of the prodigal son at a hog farm.
- Have your class help you write a book and publish it.
- Make your class a Bible college extension class for credit.
- Take your class to Palestine to see where Jesus lived.

Foster creativity with humility. We adults tend to become unteachable after a while. Our minds close to alternatives, and we become defensive of the old ways. Open-mindedness, however, allows us to learn again. It makes us flexible, and with flexibility comes creativity.

One teacher at a technical institute asked his students to measure the height of a building using a barometer. He wanted them to follow a formula for figuring height based on barometric pressure. But his students taught him new ways of doing it. One of them went to the top of the building and lowered his barometer on a string to measure the building. Another dropped his barometer off the building and timed its fall. A third climbed the stairs and measured the walls, and one creative student used his barometer to bribe the building superintendent into showing him the blueprints!

When students suggest ideas in class, write them down and consider them seriously. When you read about a new idea in a book, don't toss it aside saying, "Just another crackpot idea." Consider it. You and I are somewhat less than God. We can be wrong. We need to entertain all ideas—one of them may turn out to be a friend.

Likewise, perfectionism in the classroom is usually counterproductive. Perfectionism paralyzes performance. It causes nervous breakdowns. It's one thing to aim for a successful class but quite another to aim for a perfect class. Give yourself room for failure, and you will do better in the long run.

E. Paul Torrance studied creative teachers for many years. He noted that the most creative teachers tended to have more failures than the average teacher. The reason? They tried more things! But when they did succeed, they made an unforgettable impact on students.

Creative attitudes are the real secret of creativity, but there are also some simple techniques or "tricks" you can use to increase your teaching sparkle. Here are some of them.

Play Around

Good ideas are easier to find when you *play* than when you sweat. After playing with ideas you can sweat to put the best ones into action.

For example, if you are teaching a lesson about Adam and Eve eating the fruit in the garden, let your mind play with the scene and its possibilities.

Hold class in a garden—give everyone apples—dress up like a snake—bring a real snake to class—take an imaginary trip to the Garden of Eden—make a giant apple with a bite out of it—make fig leaf aprons—role-play the event—drive your class out of the classroom just as God drove Adam and Eve out of the garden—make a list of all the things the world says will give you wisdom and analyze the lies—teach the class in an orchard—fill the room with stuffed animals and potted plants—pantomime the story—present it as a news story with Tom Brokaw reporting—have Adam appear and tell the story for himself.

After playing around with some ideas, pick one that is most in line with your aim and play around with it some more, trying to flesh it out.

For example, take the idea of dressing up like a snake. How could you pull this off? Would you need an entire costume or just a snake's head? How about a snake puppet? Wear a garbage bag over your head?

Let's say you decide to wear a garbage bag snake head. What kind of bag? Silver? How will you put snake markings on it? Felt marker? What about fangs? Use pencils for fangs?

Work out the details bit by bit. Your final, finished idea may not, in the least, resemble your original idea, but who will know?

Research

Before Thomas Edison would invent anything, he would first go to the libraries and see if someone else had already invented it. "Why reinvent the wheel?" he thought.

Many good ideas have already been worked out, perhaps in a better way than you could have done them yourself. How can you find out?

- Visit a Christian bookstore and browse.
- Visit a Christian college library and browse.
- Send away for catalogs and free publications.
- Talk to other teachers who have been teaching longer than you.
- Visit the public school and talk to teachers.
- Attend teacher workshops in your area.
- Write to publishers for sample materials.

One of the simplest ways to prime your creative pump is to take a large catalog or magazine and go through it while asking yourself, "How can I use this for my class?" For example, the toy section of the catalog might suggest a number of classroom games that will teach and be fun at the same time.

Fantasize

In order to break your mind free from the conventional, use fantasy to explore the ridiculous. Then bring the fantasy down to earth.

For example, suppose you want to improve your classroom. Pretend that money, time, and energy are irrelevant and ask yourself to design "the world's best equipped and most lavish classroom." Your fantasies might include: thick carpeting, couches instead of chairs, remote control lighting, televisions and VCRs, computers, a drama stage, a talk show setting, study carrels, a video projector, a kitchen, marble-lined rest rooms, wall-to-wall chalkboards, oak desks, a library, piped-in music, a drinking fountain, etc. Then go over your list and see if there's anything you can use in a modified way. Maybe you can indeed start a classroom library. Play soothing music on your tape player before class. Bring in a couch. Paint an entire wall with chalkboard paint. Make one corner of the room a drama stage with curtains.

Force Fit

One particular method of creating ideas that seems to be more productive than most is a method called "force fitting" or "synectics." It involves taking what you have on hand, or what you already know about and using it for teaching, even if at first it doesn't seem to fit.

Are you a handyman with a woodworking shop? Bring tools to class to illustrate a lesson, or involve your class in building a model of Jerusalem.

Are you a nurse? Design a lesson that uses pills, shots, blood pressure cuff, etc., to teach about spiritual health.

Use what you have.

Even more importantly, use what you love, because our creativity seems to be higher in the areas where our emotions run deep. "Where your heart is, there will your creativity be."

You might sit down and make a list of all your favorite things. Your list might look something like this:

- basketball
- gift-wrapping
- eating out
- teddy bears
- shopping
- gardening
- sewing
- letter-writing

By forcing yourself to adapt what you love to your teaching, here are some ideas you might come up with.

Basketball: Arrange your lesson like a basketball game. Introduce it with a pre-game warm-up. Tip-off to start. Half-time review. Time-out for learning centers. Post-game talk to summarize and reinforce.

Teach lessons on basketball topics such as teamwork, discipline, winning and losing, practice, offense and defense, rules, etc.

Gift-wrapping: Put parts of the lesson in boxes wrapped like gifts and open them as you go through the lesson, or bring a fancy gift to class and compare it with a person—pretty, enticing, but empty inside.

Eating out: Hold a banquet lesson—students lie down to eat as they did in Bible times. Throw a party, and have students make place mats and decorations that teach. Put Bible verses in fortune cookies. Hold a wilderness wandering, a survival march through a nearby woods, or set up your class like a little restaurant and have the lesson points on a menu.

Teddy bears: Teach a lesson on what makes a good friend, using the bear as an example of security, faithfulness, etc. Let students take care of a bear for a week to teach responsibility. Use bear expressions in your lesson: "I can't bear to be without Jesus"; "Please bear with me"; "Bear ye one another's burdens." Interview a bear using a child for the voice; develop a script including questions like, "What is it like being small?"

Shopping: Give students play money, and let them decide how to spend it in an imaginary store that teaches values. Let students "clerk" booths that sell virtues. Make a Christian credit card for each student, and teach them about grace. Give students shopping coupons for memory work learned.

Gardening: Draw analogies to the Christian life such as weeds are sin, bugs are the devil, soil needs fertilizer (the Word), etc. Put lesson Scriptures on cardboard seeds inside manila envelope seed packs. Talk to students about growth, pruning, cultivating, etc.

Sewing: Let the class help you make a quilt. Make a coat of many colors for the Joseph lesson. Make a fabric version of the Ten Commandments. Do a wall hanging of the Lord's Prayer. Dye white rags purple when talking about Lydia. Make pillows decorated with Bible verses.

Letter-writing: Ask kids to write to a missionary. Let adults compose a letter to the editor of the local newspaper about some moral theme. Set up a mailbox in your classroom and promise to answer student mail. Write a *Dear Abby* column, and let students write a reply. Let students write letters to God and publish them. Write thank-you notes to other students.

Pray

Prayer is a very creative force in the world, and teachers who want to "connect" should tap the Higher Power for help. Even if prayer were not answered, it is still a valuable tool for helping us clarify our goals and for easing the strain of our work by ventilating to God.

When you pray, pray for specific needs such as "Help me know how to discipline Randy" or "Help me know when my students are ready to make a decision for Christ." Unless your prayers are specific, you will probably not recognize an answer when you see it. How would you know if God "blessed your class"? But you will be able to know when he blessed Randy with better behavior!

Make Your Creativity Work

Having good ideas is only part of the process of being creative. Ideas have to be backed up by hard work and patience. Often you will have to *sell* your ideas to other teachers or to board members. When that's the case, remember the following tips.

1. Pretest your idea if possible. Present it to a friend to see how he reacts before presenting to your class or board members.

2. Prepare others to receive your idea. Other people may not have your vision for the possibilities of your idea. You may have to show them a sample, role-play it, or show a list of materials and details.

3. Present your idea modestly. No matter how terrific your idea is, people tend to be suspicious of new ideas, especially when they are presented with wild enthusiasm. Admit to weaknesses and problems. Be realistic.

4. Go slowly. It takes time for people to get used to new ideas. Sometimes you might want to use just part of an idea. Or announce your plans way in advance so others can get used to the idea.

5. Sometimes the best ideas are first rejected, then later accepted. The initial "fizz and sputter" over a new idea will eventually die down, and the people who fought you will become your strongest allies.

Expect to have some of your ideas "stolen." It happens. Expect others to get the credit. Expect problems, expenses. But don't let any of these frustrations keep you from trying the new.

By definition, a teacher is a learner. If you are willing to blaze a trail to the future, you can also lead students into the future.

Good teaching!

Resources

Videos

Design For Teaching Young Children. Cincinnati: Standard Publishing, 1993.

Design For Teaching Children. Cincinnati: Standard Publishing, 1993.

Design For Teaching Teens. Cincinnati: Standard Publishing, 1994.

Design For Teaching That Changes Lives of Young Children. Cincinnati: Standard Publishing, 1994.

Design For Teaching That Changes Lives of Children. Cincinnati: Standard Publishing, 1994.

Design For Teaching Learners With Disabilities. Cincinnati: Standard Publishing, 1994.

Hugs and Fishes. Ventura: Gospel Light, 1991.

Molder of Dreams, Colorado Springs: Focus on the Family, 1993.

Books

Principles and Methods of Teaching

Bolte, Chuck, and Paul McCusker. *Youth Ministry Drama & Comedy*. Loveland: Group Books, 1987.

Haystead, Wes and Sheryl (editors). *Sunday School Smart Pages*. Ventura: Gospel Light, 1992.

Hendricks, Howard, and Garnet Pike. *Teaching to Change Lives*. Franklin Springs: Advocate, 1991.

Kuhlman, Edward. *Master Teacher*. Grand Rapids: Baker Books, 1987.

Miller, Paul, and Dan Dunlop. *Create a Drama Ministry*. Kansas City: Lillenas Publishing, 1984.

Shafer, Carl (editor). *Excellence in Teaching With the Seven Laws*. Grand Rapids: Baker Books, 1985.

Voges, Ken, and Ron Braund. *Understanding How Others Misunderstand You*. Chicago: Moody Press, 1990.

Wilkinson, Bruce. *Seven Laws of the Learner*. Portland: Multnomah Press, 1992.

Learner Characteristics and Needs

Adams, Dan. *The Child Influencers: Restoring the Lost Art of Parenting*. Cuyahoga Falls: Home Team Press, 1990.

Bolton, Barbara, Charles T. Smith, and Wes Haystead. *Everything You Want to Know About Teaching Children*. Ventura: Gospel Light, 1987.

Brubaker, Joanne, Robert Clark, and Roy Zuck. *Childhood Education in the Church*. Chicago: Moody, 1986.

Gangel, Kenneth O., and Howard Hendricks. *The Christian Education Handbook on Teaching*. Wheaton: Victor Books, 1988.

Haystead, Wes. *Everything You Want to Know About Teaching Young Children*. Ventura: Gospel Light, 1989.

Olson, G. Keith. *Why Teenagers Act the Way They Do*. Loveland: Group Books, 1987.

Soderholm, Marjorie E. *Understanding the Pupil* (3 parts: Preschool Child, Primary & Junior Child, Adolescent). Grand Rapids: Baker Books, 1976.

Stoop, David A. *Ways to Help Them Learn, Youth*. Ventura: Gospel Light, ICL, 1972.

Wright, H. Norman. *Ways to Help Them Learn, Adults*. Ventura: Gospel Light, ICL, 1972

Visuals

Bedell, Kenneth B. *The Role of Computers in Religious Education*. Nashville: Abingdon Press, 1986.

Clemans, E. V. *Using Computers in Religious Education*. Nashville: Abingdon Press, 1986.

Crabtree, June. *Basic Principles of Effective Teaching*. Cincinnati: Standard Publishing, 1982.

Doan, Eleanor L. *Make-it-yourself Visual Aid Encyclopedia*. Glendale: Regal Books, 1974.

Espinosa, Leonard J., and John E. Morlan. *Preparation of Inexpensive Teaching Materials*. Carthage: Fearon Teaching Aids, 1988.

Green, Lee. *Use Your Overhead*. Wheaton: Victor Books, 1979.

Lloyd, Dorothy M. *70 Activities for Classroom Learning Centers*. Dansville: The Instructor Publications, Inc., 1974.

Satterthwaite, Les. *Instructional Media: Materials, Production & Utilization*. Dubuque: Kendal/Hunt, 1990.

Satterthwaite, Les. *Audiovisual: Utilization, Production, and Design*. Dubuque: Kendal/Hunt, 1983.

Turner, Chip R. *The Church Video Answerbook*. Nashville: Broadman Press, 1991.

Creativity

Coleman, William. *You Can Be Creative*. Eugene: Harvest House, 1983.

Dorsett, Judy. *Handbook of Creativity*. Cincinnati: Standard Publishing, 1984.

Huitsing, Betty, Elsiebeth McDaniel, Betty Riley, and Mary Tucker. *Adventures in Creative Teaching*. Wheaton: Victor Books, 1986.

Richards, Lawrence O. *Creative Bible Teaching*. Chicago: Moody Press, 1970.

Von Oech, Roger. *A Whack on the Side of the Head*. New York: Warner Books, 1993.

Sunday School Organization and Management

Brown, Lowell E. *Sunday School Standards*. Ventura: Gospel Light, 1986.

Cionca, John. *The Troubleshooting Guide to Christian Education*. Denver: Accent Books, 1986.

Saifer, Steffen. *Practical Solutions for Practically Any Problem: The Early Childhood Teacher's Manual*. St. Paul: Redleaf Press, 1990.

Small Group Teaching

Arnold, Jeffrey. *The Big Book on Small Groups*. Downers Grove: InterVarsity Press, 1992.

Benson, Dennis C. *Creative Bible Studies*. Loveland: Group Books, 1985.

Nicholas, Ron (coordinator). *Good Things Come in Small Groups*. Downers Grove: InterVarsity, 1985.

Sikora, Pat. *Small Group Bible Studies: How to Lead Them*. Cincinnati: Standard Publishing, 1991.

Spade, Norma. *Your Guide to Successful Home Bible Studies*. Nashville: Thomas Nelson, 1979.

Teaching in Christian Schools

Baker, A. A. *The Successful Christian School*. Pensacola: A Beka Book Publications, 1979.

Kienel, Paul. *Reasons For Christian Schools*. Milford: Mott Media, 1981.

Influencing Public Schools

Boggs, Linden, and Joseph D. Addison. *Concerned Parents—You Can Help Your Public School*. Cincinnati: Standard Publishing, 1986.

Burron, Arnold, and John Eidsmoe. *Christ in the Classroom*. Elgin: Cook, 1987.

Herr, Ethel. *Schools: How Parents Can Make a Difference*. Chicago: Moody, 1981.

Hill, Brian V. *Faith at the Blackboard*. Grand Rapids: William B. Eerdmans, 1982.

Smith, David W. *Choosing Your Child's School*. Grand Rapids: Zondervan, 1991.

Home Schooling

Ballman, Ramond E. *The How and Why of Homeschooling*. Wheaton: Good News, 1987.

Harris, Greg. *The Christian Home School*. Brentwood: Wolgemuth & Hyatt, 1988.

Moore, Raymond and Dorothy. *Home-Grown Kids*. *Irving*: Word Books, 1984.

Moore, Raymond and Dorothy. *Homestyle Teaching*. *Irving*: Word Books, 1989.

Periodicals

Church Teachers. San Francisco: HarperCollins Publishers.

Homeschool Digest. Winona Lake: Wisdom Publishing.

Homeschooling Today. Melrose: S Squared Productions.

Key Magazine, Cincinnati: Standard Publishing.

Practical Homeschooling. Fenton: Home Life.

Teach Newsletter. Fort Worth: Sweet Publishing.

Teachers in Focus. Colorado Springs: Focus on the Family Educational Resources.

The Teaching Home. Portland: The Teaching Home.